Instant Design

Fundamentals of Autodesk Inventor® 7

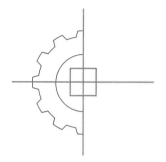

Stephen J. Ethier

Christine A. Ethier

CADInnovations

PEARSON

Prentice Hall

Upper Saddle River, New Jersey
Columbus, Ohio

Library of Congress Cataloging-in-Publication Data

Ethier, Stephen J.
    Instant design: fundamentals of Autodesk Inventor 7 / Stephen J. Ethier, Christine A. Ethier.
        p. cm.
    ISBN 0-13-114967-9
    1. Engineering graphics. 2. Inventor (Computer file). I. Title.

T353 .E88 2004
620'.0042'02855369--dc21   2003045993

Editor in Chief: Stephen Helba
Executive Editor: Debbie Yarnell
Managing Editor: Judith Casillo
Editorial Assistant: Jonathan Tenthoff
Production Editor: Louise N. Sette
Production Supervision: Lisa Garboski, *bookworks*
Design Coordinator: Diane Ernsberger
Text Designer: STELLARViSIONs
Cover Designer: Ali Mohrman
Cover Art: Stephen J. Ethier
Production Manager: Brian Fox
Marketing Manager: Jimmy Stephens

This book was set in Adobe Caslon by STELLARViSIONs. It was printed and bound by Courier Kendallville, Inc. The cover was printed by Phoenix Color Corp.

Disclaimer:

The publication is designed to provide tutorial information about AutoCAD® and/or other Autodesk computer programs. Every effort has been made to make this publication complete and as accurate as possible. The reader is expressly cautioned to use any and all precautions necessary, and to take appropriate steps to avoid hazards, when engaging in the activities described herein.

Neither the author nor the publisher makes any representations or warranties of any kind, with respect to the materials set forth in this publication, express or implied, including without limitation any warranties of fitness for a particular purpose or merchantability. Nor shall the author or the publisher be liable for any special, consequential or exemplary damages resulting, in whole or in part, directly or indirectly, from the reader's use of, or reliance upon, this material or subsequent revisions of this material.

Pearson Education Ltd.
Pearson Education Singapore Pte. Ltd.
Pearson Education Canada, Ltd.
Pearson Education—Japan

Pearson Education Australia Pty. Limited
Pearson Education North Asia Ltd.
Pearson Educación de Mexico, S. A. de C.V.
Pearson Education Malaysia Pte. Ltd.

10 9 8 7 6 5 4 3 2 1
ISBN: 0-13-114967-9

to Rob and Laura Maillet
for his quick wit, delightful humour
and gentle nature,
and for her brilliant intellect, deep emotion
and quirky view of the world...

Thank you both so much for your
friendship, your love, and the most
precious gift of both Brenna
and King Jessie the Magnificent.

Preface

Instant Design: Fundamentals of Autodesk Inventor® 7, another text in the Instant Design and Drafting series, continues the tradition of delivering technical information in a quick and easy format. Although this book does not attempt to cover all the complexities of the program, it does offer a firm grounding in the basics of part and assembly creation from sketch to production drawings.

Autodesk Inventor is a 3D, feature-based, parametric modeler that allows the user to create models of 3D parts from 2D sketches, then to use these parts to create detailed drawings and assemblies. The power of the program lies in its parametric abilities to alter an existing design to be used for a variety of applications. At any time, you can change the shape and size of the features that contain the part. And, once a part has been created, two-dimensional drawings of the part in various views can be created automatically by applying drafting standards such as hidden features and auxiliary views, as well as notations for typical features such as countersinks and counterbores.

The aim of this text is to give you information and hands-on practical experience so that you will be able to make use of this complex interface in the most efficient manner possible. To this end

- we have included hundreds of figures to illustrate the various processes needed to move from a 2D sketch to a fully annotated drawing, using a 3D solid model as the base.
- for each new process, concise theory is given, followed by a practical application to reinforce the newly obtained information.

The layout of the book is explained in Chapter 1, but we feel it is essential to re-emphasize the various components that comprise a chapter.

- The first section in each chapter lists **key ideas** that will be covered in the chapter.
- Throughout the chapter you may see a variety of things:
    - **stylized print** that lifts an idea from the pages for emphasis,
    - **tip boxes** that stress a certain fact about the program,
    - **command sequences** in a very simple, bold letter print that present the user's desired input, and
    - **Hands-On exercises** to reinforce a new idea.
- As well, at the end of each chapter you will find
    - a **short-answer test,**
    - a series of **longer answer questions,** and
    - a number of **assignments.**

Remember that the more you put into it in effort, study, and exercise completion, the more you'll take away from it in learning. It's up to you.

Take Note

It would seem you would be correct in assuming that it would be impossible to even introduce a complex subject like Autodesk Inventor in 200 pages. "How do they do it?" you are most likely asking yourself. Well, we'll share the secret at this early stage of the game. The CD-ROM that accompanies this text makes all the difference.

The CD-ROM serves as a Learning Assistant and provides you with numerous files and activities that are an integrated part of the text. The CD-ROM gives you visual help to bridge a gap in understanding. It provides the details you may need when creating drawings, and it offers hands-on reinforcement for your newly mastered skills. That's how we present so much information in 200 pages—we don't! By using the accompanying CD-ROM in concert with the text, you get the benefit of so much more.

Autodesk Inventor is a very complex and powerful program, but the experience of learning it shouldn't be dull or threatening. Rather, with lots of exercises, informal language, and friendly graphics it is easier to learn. Some topics—those you need to perform the most basic operations—are explained more fully, while others we leave for you to investigate on your own. We're sure this is the start of a journey that will bring wider horizons, lucrative results, and the pleasure that comes with mastery of a new tool.

Acknowledgments

First of all, many thanks to Stephen Helba, mentor and friend, for all his work on our behalf, and to Debbie Yarnell, a lovely young lady who manages to be in charge and flexible simultaneously, and to Judy Casillo, our technical editor/problem solver/human behavior management consultant, for many good decisions and interventions. Also, thanks to Lisa Garboski for her fine project management and to Pat Wilson for her excellent manuscript editing. And, of course, to Autodesk for their ever-prompt technical support and knowledge, we are always grateful.

Contents

Chapter 3   **Part Creation**   **51**

Chapter 4   **Viewing and Working in 3D**   **71**

Chapter 5   **Part Editing**   **95**

Chapter 6   **Part Drawing**   **119**

Chapter 7   **Assembly Creation**   **141**

Chapter 8   **Assembly Drawing**   **161**

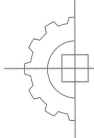

Chapter 1

Introduction to Autodesk Inventor

Key Concepts

- ◆ Autodesk Inventor Design Process
- ◆ Interacting with Autodesk Inventor
- ◆ Using the Browser

Welcome!

Welcome to *Instant Design: Fundamentals*. If you're familiar with other books in the Instant AutoCAD series, then you're already aware that we want to teach you how to use Autodesk Inventor in the fastest and most effective way possible. We want you to start using Autodesk Inventor right away, so that your confidence grows as quickly as your knowledge does.

Autodesk Inventor is a 3D, feature-based, parametric modeler. You can, therefore, create models of 3D (three-dimension) parts by making use of 2D (two-dimension) sketches. From these parts, you can create detail drawings and assemblies; Figure 1.1 illustrates the model creation progression in a simplified form.

This book is designed for those who are familiar with a 2D CAD program such as AutoCAD. If you're unfamiliar with the standard AutoCAD, you should start with our *Instant AutoCAD: Essentials* textbook. It will give you all the basics of using AutoCAD and provide you with the basis for a smooth glide into using Autodesk Inventor and this textbook. Appendix B gives you an overview of some of the basic 2D commands if you need a review. For those of you who are familiar with AutoCAD or Mechanical Desktop, Autodesk Inventor is a stand-alone program designed to operate outside AutoCAD. A comparison of Autodesk Inventor commands to AutoCAD is given in Appendix B.

In this chapter, you'll be introduced to the Autodesk Inventor design process and you'll practice interacting with Inventor toolbars and the Browser.

...Before attempting to use Autodesk Inventor, you should be familiar with the basics of drawing in a 2D CAD program such as AutoCAD.

A Brief Tour

Our goal is to provide you with background knowledge of Autodesk Inventor commands as well as to teach you the practical applications of its features. Each command or procedure introduced to you is followed, in most cases, by a hands-on, practical application. Although this hands-on approach is essential for physical learners, the concrete tasks make the experience beneficial for relational and mental learners as well.

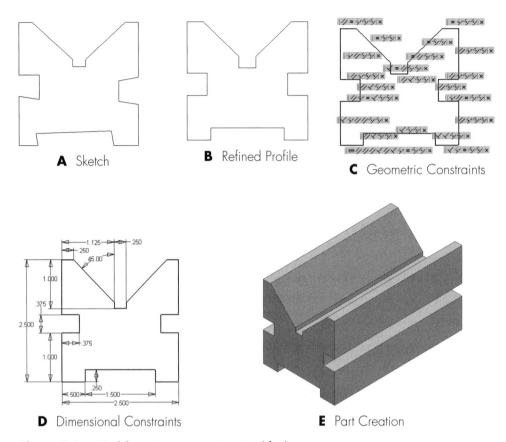

A Sketch   **B** Refined Profile   **C** Geometric Constraints

D Dimensional Constraints   **E** Part Creation

Figure 1.1   Model creation progression simplified

The hands-on sections are easily identified by the **Hands-On** heading. Any time you see **the hand**, you'll know it's time to practice using Autodesk Inventor.

You'll also notice **icons** in the left margin. These icons represent Autodesk Inventor commands that are picked from menus and help you to identify the actual commands in the program.

The **lightbulb/idea** symbol is attached to the Tip boxes throughout the text; the boxes provide tips on items that help you avoid beginner pitfalls.

Your CD-ROM includes numerous models and drawings to make learning easier and faster. Be sure to copy those into the iainv folder (subdirectory) on your computer. (Go to Appendix A if you need help making your copy.)

The end of each chapter provides you with questions and assignments to reinforce what you've learned. Some of the assignments at the end of each chapter will be used in later assignments so that you can build on what you have learned and practiced. These types of assignments are marked with a building block symbol as shown in the column next to this text. Whenever you see this symbol you know that the file created will be used later on in another assignment.

Autodesk Inventor Design Process

To create in 3D, you must understand some basic concepts and terms. To help you understand them, let's review the Autodesk Inventor design process. As you follow through this text, you will build on these concepts as we go into greater detail. For now, familiarize yourself with the following basic principles.

Projects

Autodesk Inventor uses a system of *Projects* to manage your design files. To start a new design, you create a Project. The Project contains reference to a series of folders that allow you to share libraries.

Parts and Assemblies

Ultimately your goal is to create a complete part or an assembly of parts. Autodesk Inventor operates in two environments: one for single parts (part environment), and one for parts that will be formed into assemblies (assembly environment). You will begin to learn how to use Autodesk Inventor by using the single-part mode. Once you're comfortable, you'll move on to creating assemblies. Figure 1.2 shows a part and an assembly.

Parametric Design

When you create a part, you determine the size, shape, and position of its various features. By assigning editable numeric values for size, shape, and position, you can alter the design of the part at any time for a variety of functions. This ability to alter the design is referred to as parametric design. Figure 1.3 shows a single part with its design altered by changing the values of its features.

> By assigning editable numeric values for size, shape, and position, you can alter the design of the part at any time for a variety of functions.

Figure 1.2 Single part and assembly

A

B

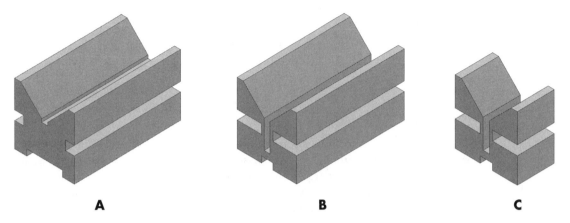

Figure 1.3   A part altered through parametric design

Feature Driven

A part is created through the use of specific features that describe its shape. This is referred to as feature driven. The features are the 3D shapes that form the part. Features are created through actions such as revolve, extrude, and sweep, using profiles shown in Figure 1.4. There are also standard features such as holes and fillets that can be added.

Profiles and Sketches

Profiles are the shapes that can be turned into features through such actions as extrude or revolve. Profiles are one of the most significant elements of the part design. To create a profile, you first sketch it roughly and then turn it into a refined profile with constraints. Constraints control the shape (geometric) and size (dimensional) of the profile. This is another application of parametric design. Figure 1.5 shows an initial sketch and the profile with constraints.

Detail Drawings

Once your part is completed, you can use it to create fully annotated (notes and dimensions) multiview drawings as shown in Figure 1.6. These drawings are created with a base view and other views *based* on it. Dimensions and notes are applied through automatic and manual means.

Figure 1.4   A part created with specific features

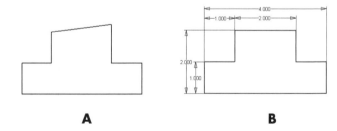

Figure 1.5   Profile created from a sketch

Figure 1.6 Detail drawing created from 3D part

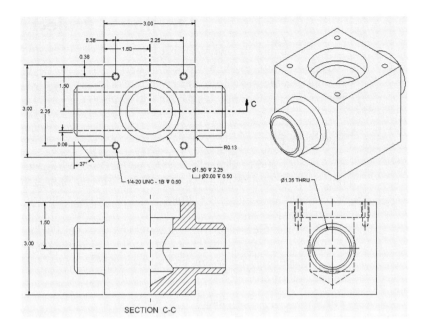

Assembly Drawings

Assembly drawings can be created with a variety of views including exploded views as shown in Figure 1.7; exploded assembly views are created through the use of presentation views. Part balloons and bills of materials (BOMs) can also be added.

Advanced Features

There are a number of advanced features that can be used to enhance your design. Table-driven iParts that use a spreadsheet can create from one part a variety of standard parts such as nuts and bolts. Engineer's Notebook and Design Assistant are two more advanced features of Autodesk Inventor. These topics are not covered in the main body of this text but some information is included in the Appendices.

Figure 1.7
Assembly drawing showing part balloons and bill of materials

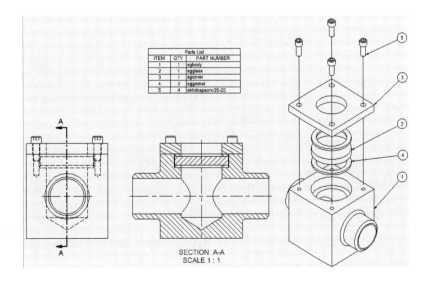

Starting a Project

In the beginning you may feel that there are a lot of steps to a design project, but once you've gone through the procedure once or twice, you'll see that it's not difficult at all. In this section we're going to review how you begin a project and start designing. The Hands-On at the end of this section will give you a practical application of the theory.

Project File

Setting up a Project file is the starting point. Autodesk Inventor uses projects to logically organize files and to maintain valid links between files. A project consists of a project home folder/directory and a project file that specifies the paths and locations of the files in the project.

A project file is a text file with an .ipj extension. It's located in the home folder for the project. The file specifies the paths to the files in the project.

A single project may contain numerous files. Some of the different file types that you will encounter are:

File type	Extension	Description
Project	.ipj	The location of your design files
Part	.ipt	A single part
Assembly	.ipa	A group of parts integrated to form an assembly
Drawing	.idw	A layout that contains views of a part or assembly
Presentations	.ipn	An exploded view of an assembly
Design Views	.idv	A custom view of an assembly

The procedure to set up a project can be as simple as specifying in which folder your files will be located. Whenever you start a new design, it will automatically be located in the proper project folder.

Drawing Templates

There's a template file for each type of design element in a project. A template file contains all the initial settings required to perform a specific task. For instance, if you create a part, you would use the part template; the settings and menus are configured for part creation. Later, when you want to produce a drawing, you would use a drawing template; this time the settings and menus are configured for drawing creation. Using this method can lead to faster learning of the program because you're presented with only the appropriate tools for the task. You won't have to wade through numerous commands that don't apply to what you want to do.

To make it easier to identify the different templates and file types, Autodesk Inventor uses a different icon to represent the file type of which there are three groupings: Default, English, and Metric. The default templates use the units that were specified when the program was initially installed on the computer. Figure 1.8 shows the different icons and the associated file type.

Part	Assembly	Drawing	Presentation	Sheet Metal	Weldment
Standard (in).ipt	Standard (in).iam	ANSI (in).idw	Standard.ipn	Sheet Metal (in).ipt	Weldment (ANSI).iam

Figure 1.8   Identifying file icons—English templates: (a) Part, (b) Assembly, (c) Drawing, (d) Presentation, (e) Sheet Metal, and (f) Weldment

You should pay particular attention to the fact that the standard part file and the sheet metal file use the same icon. This is because they're basically the same part. However, they do have different settings and you cannot change from one to the other. So, take care to choose the proper file template when starting.

You can also create your own templates by simply saving a specific file type in the template file folder. This way you can customize templates for your projects. They can contain geometry; for instance, you can create a drawing template file that contains your drawing title block.

Hands-On: Starting a Project and Navigating the Screen

In this exercise you'll start a new project, begin a design, and review the layout of the screen (User Interface—UI). If you need a refresher on the use of 2D CAD, refer to Appendix C. It explains some of the basic 2D commands and also has a comparison between Autodesk Inventor and AutoCAD commands.

1.   Start Autodesk Inventor by:

Autodesk Inventor 6

a. locating the Autodesk Inventor shortcut icon and double-clicking it, or

b. picking the Windows™ Start button, entering the Programs submenu, finding the Autodesk Inventor menu, and picking the Autodesk Inventor menu item.

The Autodesk Inventor splash screen will appear momentarily and be replaced with the Open dialog box as shown in Figure 1.9. Note the three tabs at the top of the dialog box: Default, English, and Metric. As explained earlier, these decide which unit of measure your design will use during creation.

Figure 1.9 Open dialog box

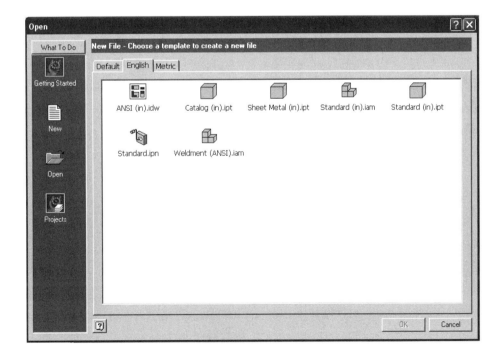

Creating a Project

2.   Pick the Projects icon. The dialog box now shows the Projects window as shown in Figure 1.10(a).

The upper portion of the window lists the various projects. Depending on your system, there may be more or fewer projects listed.

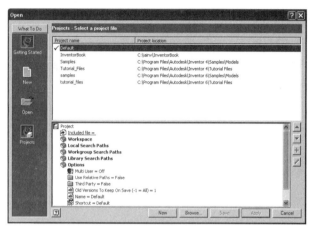

A

B

C

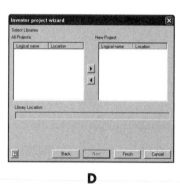

D

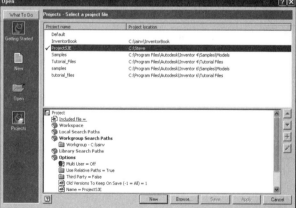

E

Figure 1.10   Starting a project

The lower portion of the screen gives information about the project. Highlight one of the projects in the upper list and observe the information in the lower list. Note the folder names for locations of files.

3.   You're now going to create a project. *Note:* Ask your instructor if you have permission to create a project folder on your system. If you're on a network, you may have permission to create folders only in certain locations.

Pick the New button at the bottom of the Projects screen; the Inventor Project Wizard dialog box appears as shown in Figure 1.10(b). Make sure your settings match the figure. You're creating a new project; however, it will use existing files.

Once you've checked the settings, pick the Next button. The next window appears as shown in Figure 1.10(c). Enter your project name, such as ProjectSJE (use your initials to identify your project as in SJE).

To set the location for your project, you can type in the location for a new folder or use the Browse button to locate an existing folder where your files are stored. As mentioned at the beginning of this step, your instructor may want you to start your project in a personal folder.

Next, set the location of the existing files. This is used when you want to use parts or assemblies from another project for your new project. For this book, set the location of the existing files to the location where you copied the files from the CD-ROM. If you followed the procedure in Appendix A, you've already copied the files that came with this book into the c/:iainv folder.

Once this is complete, press the Next button to continue. The Select Libraries window appears (Figure 1.10(d)). If you had a library of parts you wanted to use on your project, you would highlight the desired library on the All Projects side and use the arrow button to copy it to the New Project side. In this case there are no libraries to use. Pick the Finish button to complete the creation of the project. If the project path/folder doesn't exist, you'll automatically be prompted to create it. Usually you respond by picking the OK button.

4.   The Projects window now appears with your new project added to the list (Figure 1.10(e)). Double-click it to move the checkmark to alongside your project name. This makes it the active project. Review the lower portion of the window where the Workgroup shows the c:\iainv folder. You're ready to start creating some parts.

Starting a Part

5.   Pick the New icon. The New File window, which lists the various templates you can use in your project, appears.

6.   Pick the English tab to start files that will use inches as the units.

Standard (in).ipt

7.   Pick the Standard [in].ipt part template icon to start a new part file. The Autodesk Inventor program should now start and the screen should look similar to Figure 1.11.

8.   Get to know the layout of the Autodesk Inventor Part screen. Look at your screen and the following text, but do *not* exit Autodesk Inventor.

Figure 1.11
Inventor Part screen
layout

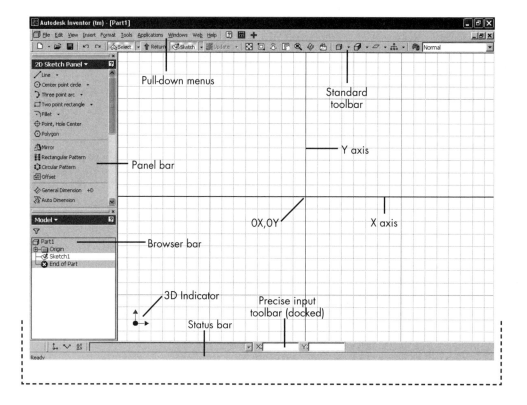

Context Menu

Get in the habit of using the right-click context menu to perform functions. When you right-click, a menu appears on the screen, giving you a series of options or commands. A context menu is intuitive. This means that it will present commands or options based on what you're doing.

Interacting with Autodesk Inventor

The screen is divided into two main user elements: the application window and the graphics window. The applications window contains the pull-down menus, command bar, docked toolbars, and command panels. The graphics window contains the modeling environment. You can have multiple graphics windows, each displaying different modeling environments. One window could display a single part, while another displays an entire assembly.

When you start a new part, the pull-down menus and toolbars are customized for the part modeling environment. Since the first stage in creating a part is to sketch the shape of the part, Autodesk Inventor automatically goes into Sketch mode. There will be more detailed information on tools and commands given in later chapters. The purpose of this section is to provide an overview.

2D CAD

For those of you who are new to CAD and CAD terminology, you may want to review Appendix C, which contains basic CAD terminology. For those of you who are familiar with AutoCAD or Mechanical Desktop, you may want to review Appendix B for the comparison between AutoCAD commands and Autodesk Inventor.

Pull-Down Menus

The pull-down menus lie at the top of the Autodesk Inventor application window. Even though they contain various commands, you'll probably find yourself using a toolbar, panel bar, or context menu for most of your commands. The pull-down menu heads may stay the same between different modeling environments, such as part modeling or assembly modeling, but their contents change with the different environments.

Toolbars

Autodesk Inventor uses a series of toolbars to perform most of the commands. Only those toolbars relevant to the active graphics window and environment are displayable. To display or hide a toolbar, you can use the View/Toolbar pull-down menu item or right-click on a blank spot on a toolbar to bring up the context menu. You can also drag toolbars around the application window to arrange them in a format that suits you.

Standard Toolbar   This toolbar contains more of the general commands used throughout Autodesk Inventor. Such items as file handling, general editing, and view commands are contained here.

You may want to pay particular note to the Undo and Redo tools. These buttons allow you to undo incorrect procedures or to redo a procedure you mistakenly undid.

The Standard toolbar now controls selection modes, sketch modes, and element style. The status bar at the bottom of the screen also gives you information on active commands.

Precise Input Toolbar   This toolbar allows precise XY positioning of a point, either with absolute values from the 0,0 origin point, or relative (delta) distances from a previous point.

It also allows you to establish a temporary relative origin point. Subsequent coordinate inputs are measured relative to the temporary origin until you change it or turn it off.

The Precise Input toolbar is not displayed by default. As a beginner you should display the toolbar and drag it to the bottom of the screen. You can display the toolbar by picking View/Toolbar/Precise Input. If there's a checkmark beside the menu item, it's on.

Panel Bar   This bar contains tool groupings for specific operations. For instance, if you were sketching a profile, the tools presented would be for sketching; if you were generating a part, the tools would be for creating features. Note the small triangle to the right of the panel bar label. Picking it displays a flyout menu, giving you a choice of which panel bar to display.

Browser Bar   This contains the structure of the generation of the parts and assemblies. You can use it to alter the order and edit elements in a design. More on the Browser bar is explained later in this chapter.

Status Bar   This bar simply gives you information on active commands.

Other Toolbars   There are other toolbars that you can display, such as 2D Sketch Panel and Part Features. As you become more familiar with Autodesk Inventor, you'll decide which toolbars you'd like visible and what arrangement you prefer. To display other toolbars, select the Tools/Customize pull-down menu and open the Toolbars tab. You can highlight any toolbar in the presented list and then pick the Show button to display it on the screen. Note that tools are "grayed-out" if they won't operate. This depends on the current modeling procedure that is active.

Graphics Screen

The graphics screen is a three-dimensional environment in which creation takes place using the Cartesian coordinate system. There are three axes to contend with: X, Y, and Z. If you're familiar with 2D CAD, you know about the Cartesian coordinate system and the X and Y axes. These are your common two-dimensional axes. The addition of the Z axis gives you the third dimension.

3D Indicator   Inside this 3D environment, you can move and create in 3D space. It's important that you keep track of your three-dimensional orientation. To help you with this is the 3D Indicator, initially found at the bottom-left corner of the graphics screen.

The 3D Indicator is composed of three directional indicators, each one formed from a line and an arrowhead and each in a different color. The green indicator line lies on the Y axis and the arrowhead points in a positive direction, the red indicator line lies on the X axis pointing in a positive direction, and the blue indicator line lies on the Z axis pointing in a positive direction.

In 2D it's shown as an L shape with the green Y and red X indicator lines. The blue Z indicator shows as a blue circle because it is pointing toward the user, perpendicular to the screen.

If the view is rotated in three dimensions, the 3D Indicator takes on the three-line indicator shape as shown in the left margin.

To display or hide the 3D Indicator, pick the Tools/Applications Options pull-down menu item. Under the General tab, there is a Show 3D Indicator box. If it's checked, the 3D Indicator is turned on (visible).

Grid   When you start a new part, the screen automatically goes into Sketch mode. By default, a grid appears on the screen to assist you with creation by giving you a visual indicator of distance. Look at your screen or Figure 1.11. Note the thicker crossing lines in the center of the screen. These represent the X and Y axes. The 0X,0Y origin point is located at the intersection of the thicker crossing lines. This is a good indicator to keep track of, especially when you need a frame of reference during creation. The gird can be turned on or off by selecting the Tools/Applications Options menu item. In the Options dialog box, under the Sketch tab, you'll find a Display section. Under this section you can control the grid display.

Cursor   As with practically any computer design program, the cursor is used to select elements (objects) and locate coordinate points. In the graphics screen, you'll find that small symbols appear next to or in the center of the cursor. These are indicators or cues telling you that an option can occur during the operation.

For example, when you're sketching a series of lines, the perpendicular symbol appears next to the cursor if the line you're drawing is perpendicular to another line in your sketch. Look at the image on the left of this text. Note the filled-in circle in the center of the cursor; this represents the endpoint of the line.

Hands-On: Moving About the Screen

1.   The Autodesk Inventor application should be running with a New Part file open and in Sketch mode. This is the last step in your previous Hands-On. You're going to practice moving around the screen and accessing commands.

For the beginning portions of this textbook, you are going to work in Part mode. This simplifies the process somewhat by eliminating any references to assemblies. Don't worry; you can always combine parts into assemblies later on.

2.   Look at the Panel bar with the heading 2D Sketch Panel. It contains all the commands you'll use in the creation of 2D sketches.

Pick the 2D Sketch Panel heading; a flyout menu appears listing the various panels you can display. Note that the Expert menu item doesn't have a checkmark beside it. Pick the Expert menu item and see what happens. When you turn Expert mode on, the description of the tools disappears so that you can see all the tools at once instead of having to scroll to find them. For now, turn Expert off by picking the 2D Sketch Panel heading and picking the Expert menu item to remove the checkmark.

3.   Move your cursor onto the New tool at the left of the Standard toolbar and pause. Note how there's a down arrow next to the New tool. Pick the down arrow. A flyout menu appears showing the various new modeling environments you can start. These are all default drawing templates. Pick the arrow again to close the flyout.

Now pick the New tool. The Open dialog box appears, allowing you access to all the drawing templates. This is the method we'll use to start new drawings for this book because we want you to work in English units for now. Pick the Cancel button to close the Open dialog box.

4.   Let's take a look at what's inside some of the pull-down menus.

Open the View pull-down menu and review the listed menu items. With the View pull-down menu open, look at it and the Standard toolbar. Note that many of the viewing tools in the View pull-down menu are also in the Standard toolbar, allowing quicker access.

Open the Tools pull-down menu and review the listed menu items. Note the various measurement tools. Pick the Document Settings menu item at the bottom of the Tools pull-down menu. The Document Settings dialog box for the current part (Part1) appears. Pick the Sketch tab (see Figure 1.12).

Figure 1.12   Sketch tab of the Document Settings dialog box

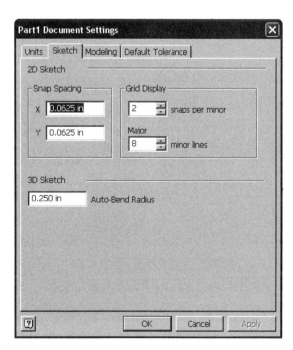

The Snap Spacing section is used to control accurate movement of the cursor. By default, it's set to 0 .0625 (or 1/16 inch). To force the cursor to only move in increments of the snap spacing, you need to turn Snap to Grid on. We'll show you how to do that in a moment. Pick the Cancel button to exit the dialog box with no changes.

5.   Now look at the Standard toolbar again. At the far right of the bar is a box that currently reads Normal. Pick the down arrow next to the box to reveal the two settings: Normal and Construction. They control the type of sketch elements you'll use. Normal refers to normal sketching, the one that's used to create a part. Construction is used for elements that won't be in the part but help to create the sketch. For now it should be left as Normal.

Near the far left of the bar is the Select button. When it's depressed it means you can select elements to modify. Pick the down arrow next to the button. You can set the priority when selecting elements: sketch, face, or feature. For now, leave it as sketch.

6.   One last thing to try during this session is turning the Panel and Browser off and on. This can be useful when you want to have a larger graphics screen to view.

Locate the ✕ in the right corner of both bars. Pick them to turn them off. To turn them back on, move your cursor to any spot on the Standard toolbar.

Right-click to bring up the toolbar context menu. Pick the Browser bar menu item first. Right-click again to bring up the toolbar context menu. Pick the Panel bar menu item last. They both should be on the screen docked at the left of the screen as shown in Figure 1.11. You'll probably need to resize them by picking and dragging on a horizontal edge of the bars.

Browser

The Browser keeps track of all the features used in sequence to create a part, and all of the parts that combine in an assembly with their 3D constraint relationships. You can modify parts and assemblies with the browser. Figures 1.13(a) and (b) show the browsers for the Part environment and the Assembly environment. One browser per session handles both the part and the assemblies. Between the environments, the browser changes slightly.

Figure 1.13
(a) Part environment and (b) Assembly environment browsers

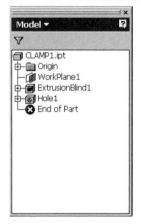

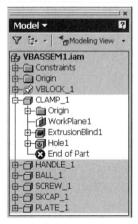

A   B

Since your first exposure is going to be to single parts, we will concentrate on the browser for the Part environment. Both browser environments operate basically the same way except for the added functions in the Assembly environment, which will be explained in Chapter 7 of this book.

Using Browser

When you start your first sketch, a part is automatically named, numbered, and represented in the browser. Because the sketch is the first step, it is nested first under the part name (see Figure 1.14(a)). As you add more features, these are added to the part to form a hierarchy, which shows the process used to design the part (see Figure 1.14(b)).

> **When you start your first sketch, a part is automatically named, numbered, and represented in the browser.**

Expanding and Collapsing Hierarchy Levels

You can expand or collapse hierarchy levels by using the plus (+) or minus (−) sign. You can collapse the entire hierarchy by right-clicking the part name and choosing Collapse from the menu.

Browser Commands

Access most of the Browser commands by either right-clicking on the part heading (Figure 1.15(a)) or right-clicking on a subheading/element (Figure 1.15(b)).

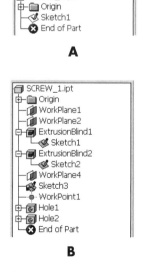

Figure 1.14   Using Browser

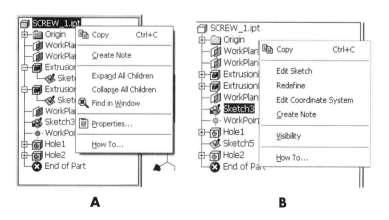

Figure 1.15   Browser cursor menus

Projects

Open

Hands-On: Using Browser

1.   If Autodesk Inventor is already open, close it and start again. This is necessary anytime you want to switch projects.

When the Open dialog box appears, pick the Projects icon and make sure your project has a checkmark beside it. If it doesn't, double-click on the project name; the checkmark should now move to beside your project.

With your project highlighted, review the project information in the lower portion of the dialog box. The Workgroup should have been set to c:/iainv. If it isn't, you'll need to create the project again with the proper path as described in the first Hands-On in this chapter.

2.   Pick the Open icon. The window changes to show the files listed in the c:/iainv folder as shown in Figure 1.16. Find the file VBLOCK1 and double-click it to open it. Look at the Browser now. It should look similar to Figure 1.17a. The part name is the same as the file name: VBLOCK1.

3.   At this stage, we want you to save this file under a new name so that you don't loose the original. Pick File/Save Copy As. The Save Copy As dialog box appears. In the File name box change VBLOCK1 to MYVBLOCK and pick Save.

4.   Close the VBLOCK1 file and open the MYVBLOCK file. Look at the browser now. It should now look similar to Figure 1.17(a). The part name is the same as the file name: MYVBLOCK. You can change the name of a part by saving it to a new file. It's very important to keep track of your part/drawing file names. They're used to create assemblies and lists of parts used in an assembly.

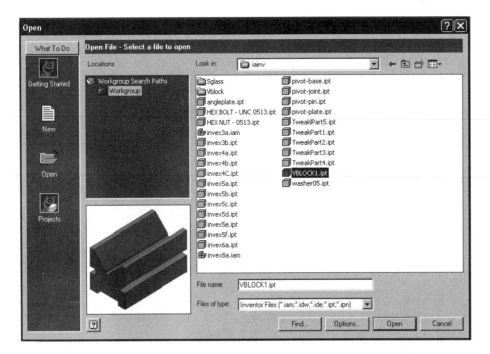

Figure 1.16   Open dialog box showing files contained in the C:/iainv folder

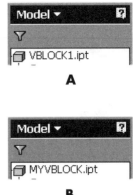

Figure 1.17
Browser part name as (a) VBLOCK1 and (b) MYVBLOCK

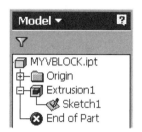

Figure 1.18
Opening levels in the
browser

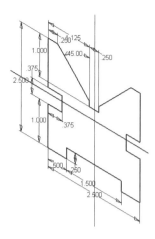

Figure 1.19 Displaying
the profile

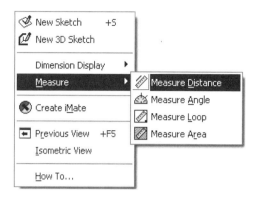

Figure 1.20   Context menu showing the
Measure options

When you name a part, it should normally be representative of the object you're creating.

5. Move your cursor into the browser and onto the boxed plus (+) sign next to the Extrusion1 level. Pick the plus sign to open up the level as shown in Figure 1.18. Under this you will find Sketch1. This is the original profile used to create the part.

6. Double-click the icon next to the name Sketch1. The part disappears to reveal the profile (see Figure 1.19). The profile also has parametric dimensions on it. These are used to control the size and shape of the profile.

7. To get the part back, we need to update it even though we haven't made any changes. Pick the Update tool, located in the Command toolbar.

8. Move your cursor into open space in the graphics window and pick. This ensures that no element is highlighted. Now, right-click to bring up the context menu as shown in Figure 1.20. On the menu, select Measure to open the flyout and then select Measure Distance. The Measure Distance dialog box appears on the screen. Note that there's a little symbol of a scale/ruler next to the cursor.

Move the cursor to one of the corners of the part and pause. You'll see a small yellow circle appear exactly on the corner. When measuring, it automatically snaps to the end or edge of a feature. Pick the corner to start the measurement and then pick another corner to finish the measurement. The measured values are now displayed in the Measure Distance dialog box. You can keep measuring until you close the dialog box by picking the × in the upper-right corner of the dialog box.

9. Before you finish this session, close the various levels in Browser by picking the minus (−) signs.

10. Save this part as MYVBLOCK. Quit Autodesk Inventor.

In a Nutshell

As you can probably tell, you can access commands in several ways: from the context menus, by selecting toolbar icons, and by selecting options from pull-down menus. Which method you use is up to you. Throughout this text we will identify the tools and the pull-down menu access to most of the commands so that you are familiar with both.

You have now gone over the initial concepts for creating models using Autodesk Inventor. You should be comfortable moving around the menus and screen, and be able to open an existing part and start a new part. Once you're ready, move on to Chapter 2.

 # Testing ... testing ... 1, 2, 3

Fill-in-the-Blanks

1. To create a profile, first make a(n) _____ and then turn it into a refined profile with _____ .
2. The most common methods of accessing commands in Autodesk Inventor are _____ and _____ .
3. There is a(n) _____ file for each type of design element in a project.

True or False

4. A project file is a text file with an .ipr extension.   T or F
5. Autodesk Inventor uses a system of projects to manage your design files.
   T or F

Multiple Choice

6. You can collapse an entire part hierarchy by
   a. clicking the minus (−) sign.
   b. right-clicking the part and choosing Collapse from the menu.
   c. left-clicking the part and choosing Collapse from the menu.
   d. all of the above
7. In Inventor, your ultimate goal is to create a(n)
   a. part.
   b. assembly.
   c. part and an assembly.
   d. part or an assembly.

 # What?

1. Name and explain the purpose of the two different environments in Inventor.

2. List the six main types of file types.

3. What's the purpose of Browser?

4. Name two of the three possible methods for accessing commands in Inventor.

5. Explain the purpose of the Panel bar and the Browser bar.

 # Let's Get Busy!

1. Practice using Browser by opening the following part and assembly files: CLAMP1, SKCAP1, VBASSEM1.

   Open and close different levels. Experiment by right-clicking when you have an item highlighted in the browser. What happens to the part on the graphics screen when you highlight it in the browser?

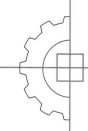

Chapter 2

Design Fundamentals

Key Concepts

- ◆ Viewing
- ◆ Sketching
- ◆ Geometric Constraints
- ◆ Dimensional Constraints
- ◆ Paths
- ◆ Sketch Doctor

Where to Begin

Usually with any design project you start by jotting down your ideas onto paper. Then, as you delve deeper into the design, you refine those initial sketches into more refined drawings. Autodesk Inventor uses the same procedure. Sketching is the first step in the design process. Your sketches, once they are turned into a refined profile, are used as building blocks that initially control the shape of the part you want to create. With this profile you can apply geometric rules (commonly called constraints) to control its shape, and dimensional constraints to control its size. This chapter deals with viewing, sketching, and applying geometric and dimensional constraints.

Viewing

Before we get started with sketching, it's important that you are able to navigate the graphics screen. If you're familiar with AutoCAD or another CAD program, then you already know viewing terminology. Here we'll explain Autodesk Inventor's method of viewing. The Hands-On will give you some practice.

Viewing Tools

The Viewing tools are located in the center of the Standard toolbar. You can use Viewing tools to manipulate the view while performing other operations. For example, if you are sketching a profile and want to get a closer view, you could use the Zoom Window tool to get a closer look while still drawing a line. The following is a description of the various Viewing tools.

 Zoom All   Zooms a view so that all the elements in the model fit in the graphics window. In a drawing layout, the active sheet fits the window.

 Zoom Window   Allows the user to specify the area to enlarge to fit within the graphics window. The cursor changes to a crosshair to be used to indicate the opposite corners of the zoom window.

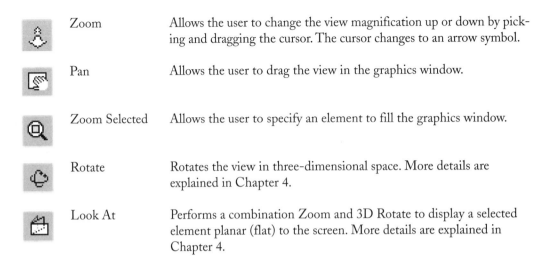

	Zoom	Allows the user to change the view magnification up or down by picking and dragging the cursor. The cursor changes to an arrow symbol.
	Pan	Allows the user to drag the view in the graphics window.
	Zoom Selected	Allows the user to specify an element to fill the graphics window.
	Rotate	Rotates the view in three-dimensional space. More details are explained in Chapter 4.
	Look At	Performs a combination Zoom and 3D Rotate to display a selected element planar (flat) to the screen. More details are explained in Chapter 4.

Display Mode

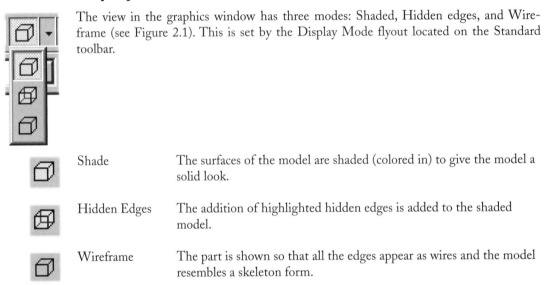

The view in the graphics window has three modes: Shaded, Hidden edges, and Wireframe (see Figure 2.1). This is set by the Display Mode flyout located on the Standard toolbar.

	Shade	The surfaces of the model are shaded (colored in) to give the model a solid look.
	Hidden Edges	The addition of highlighted hidden edges is added to the shaded model.
	Wireframe	The part is shown so that all the edges appear as wires and the model resembles a skeleton form.

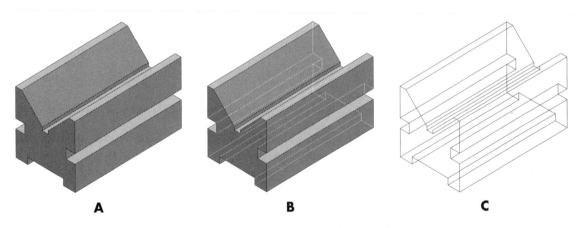

Figure 2.1   Display modes: (a) Shade, (b) Hidden edges, and (c) Wireframe

Figure 2.2
View modes:
(a) Orthographic and
(b) Perspective

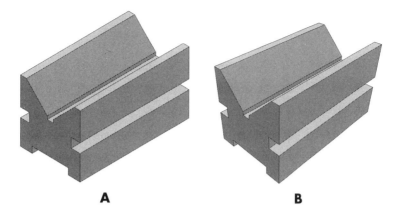

A   B

View Mode

There are two view modes: Orthographic camera mode and Perspective camera mode (see Figure 2.2). This is set by the View Mode flyout located on the Standard toolbar.

 Orthographic camera mode

Displays the model so that all its points project along parallel lines to their positions on the screen. This mode is used for most construction because it makes it easier to compare relative positions of elements.

 Perspective camera mode

Displays the model using three-point perspective. Features that are farther away appear smaller. This mode is used mainly for presentation because the way the drawing appears simulates viewing by the human eye.

Hands-On: Viewing

In this Hands-On you'll practice the various viewing commands until you're comfortable with manipulating the graphics screen.

1.   Open the part file invex2A (Chapter 2, Exercise A) from the c:\iainv folder. It contains the vblock part. The part should fill the screen. If it doesn't, pick the Zoom All tool.

Save a copy of the part using the File/Save Copy As pull-down menu command so that the original file remains unchanged. Save the copy as ex2A. Close the original invex2A file and open the ex2A file.

2.   To get a closer view of the end of the vblock, pick the Zoom Window tool and pick two opposite points to create the zoom window. Figure 2.3 shows the screen after using the Zoom Window tool.

Figure 2.3   Getting a closer look with Zoom Window

3.   Use the Pan tool to pick and drag on the screen until you see the other end of the part. To end the command, right-click and pick Done from the context menu.

4.   Use the Zoom tool to practice zooming in and out by dragging. Pick the tool, then pick in the graphics screen and drag up and down. Zoom out until the part is very small. To end the command, right-click and pick Done from the context menu.

5.   Pick the Zoom All tool to enlarge the part until it fills the screen.

6.   Pick each of the Shade Mode tools to see the effect on the part. Remember to pick and hold to see the various tools, and then drag the cursor down to select the tool.

7.   Pick each of the Display Mode tools to see the effect. Remember to pick and hold to see the various tools, and then drag the cursor down to select the tool.

8.   Repeat the above commands until you're familiar with the various viewing tools.

9.   Save your ex2A file.

Sketching

Sketches are used to create profiles and paths. Profiles are used to define the shape of the part and are created from closed sketches; the others in the preceding list use open sketches. The following information deals mainly with profile sketches, but the techniques can be applied to all the other forms of sketches. Paths may be closed or open and are explained at the end of this chapter.

Your sketches, once they are turned into a profile, are used as building blocks that initially control the shape of the part you want to create.

Sketching Tools

To generate a sketch, use the Sketch panel bar or the Sketch toolbar to create a rough outline of the part you want to create. To use a sketch tool, pick it in the Panel bar. It becomes "pushed-in" to show that it is active (see Figure 2.4). Observe the Message box in the Command toolbar. It tells you what to do next, such as to "select first corner" if you are drawing a rectangle element.

Figure 2.4   Sketch panel bar with Two-point Rectangle command active

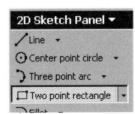

Deleting Elements

To delete a sketch element, pick the element to highlight it and right-click to bring up the context menu. Pick Delete from the menu. Another method is to highlight the element and press the Del key.

To exit a Sketch command, pick the Select tool to "push it in" to activate it or press the Esc key. The Sketch command tool should "pop out" to show it's not active.

Note that objects that are used to draw a sketch, such as lines, arcs, or circles, are referred to as elements. The tools used to modify or edit a sketch are explained in a later section in this chapter.

Sketching

Before starting your sketch, assess the look of the finished part and decide what basic profile can be used to create that part. Figure 2.5(a) shows the V-Block. Analyzing the shape of the V-Block, you can easily tell what basic profile can be used as the basis of the part, as shown in Figure 2.5(b).

The most important rule for the beginner is to keep your sketches simple. The simpler the profile, the easier it is to constrain it. If you start with an overly complex sketch you will find you have to apply many geometric and dimensional constraints to fully solve the shape. And believe us, that can get quite confusing.

When you initially draw the sketch, it is not necessary to draw it to the exact size you want; however, you will find your job easier if your initial sketch has a profile with somewhat correct proportions and close to the size you will finally want. The use of a grid can help with maintaining proportions for your sketch.

The shapes used to form the outline should not overlap each other and you should not leave a gap between objects that is more than the current pickbox size (see Figure 2.6).

The most important rule for the beginner is to keep your sketches simple.

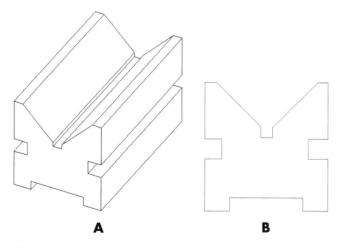

A   **B**

Figure 2.5   (a) V-Block and (b) its base feature

Figure 2.6   Examples of incorrect sketches with crossing geometry and geometry with a gap

Rough Sketching versus Exact Sketching

As a beginnner, you may find it is easier to draw your sketch to the exact size and shape to start with. This will make it much easier to constrain the profile because it has already been drawn correctly. Once you are more comfortable and proficient, you may try sketching more inexactly.

The sketch should be a continuous outline of the shape you want. Autodesk Inventor allows you to have a combination of an exterior sketch shape and interior sketch shapes to create the final profile.

Linetypes

There are three linetype styles you can use to sketch with: normal, construction, and centerline. Normal is used for normal sketching where the lines are used to create the profile. Construction is used when you want to reference geometry that's not part of the profile but will be used to create the sketch feature. An axis line used for revolving the profile is one example of a construction line. A centerline can be used for an axis of rotation but more often a construction line is used instead.

Sketching Assistants

There are some settings you should check before sketching that can be of assistance.

Document Settings

The Document Settings dialog box controls units, 2D sketching, and 3D sketching. To open the dialog box, select the Tools/Document Settings pull-down menu item. Figure 2.7 shows two of the panels in the Documents Settings dialog box.

As mentioned in Chapter 1, you can control the cursor's movements with Snap and Grid. Snap sets the actual increments that the cursor can move and Grid sets the visual indicators.

The Units tab can be used to check that you're working in the correct units. It also controls the display precision for dimensions applied to the sketch.

The Sketch tab controls the increment movement of the cursor by setting the Snap Spacing values along the X and Y spacing. When Snap is turned on, the cursor will move only in increments set in Snap Spacing. The Grid Display section is used to give you a visual indicator of distance by drawing grid lines at different intervals. The Snaps per Minor value causes a light gray line to appear every so many snap distances. The Major value displays a darker gray line every so many minor lines. Remember that the black lines are the X and Y axes that pass through 0,0.

To turn Snap to Grid on, with no command active, right-click in open space in the graphics window. The context menu appears. If there is a checkmark, Snap to Grid is on. Pick the menu item to toggle it on or off.

The Modeling tab in the Document Settings dialog box is used to control 3D sketching, which we will not go into now.

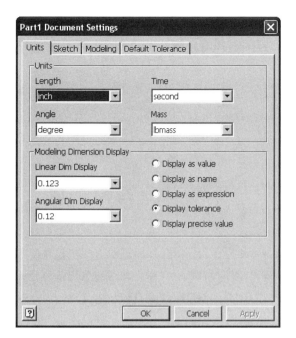
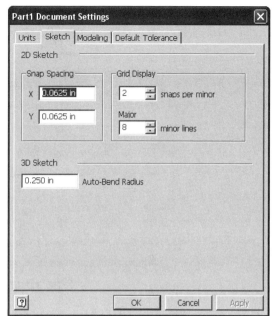

Figure 2.7   Document Settings dialog boxes

Application Options

The Options dialog box contains some settings that control sketching. To access the dialog box, select the Tools/Application Options pull-down menu and pick the Sketch tab (see Figure 2.8). For the beginner, leave the settings as shown in Figure 2.8. The only change you may need to make is to turn the grid lines on or off.

Implied Constraints

When you start sketching, implied constraints are active. What this means is if you draw a line that is almost horizontal, a horizontal constraint is automatically applied. You can tell what implied constraint is going to be applied by the cursor symbol. Figure 2.9 shows the cursor symbols for some of the implied constraints.

Figure 2.8   Sketch tab of the Options dialog box

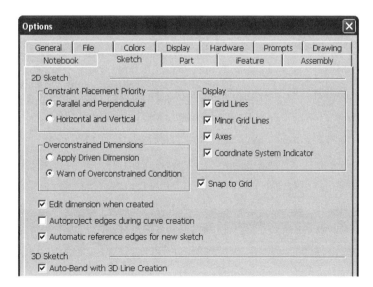

Figure 2.9   Implied
Constraints

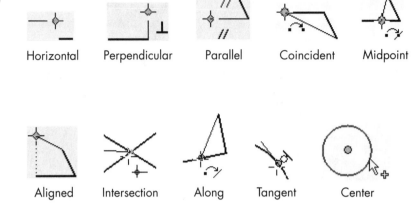

Horizontal   Perpendicular   Parallel   Coincident   Midpoint

Aligned   Intersection   Along   Tangent   Center

Disabling Implied Constraints

If you want to sketch some elements without having implied constraints, press and hold the Ctrl key while drawing the element.

Precise Input Toolbar

A very easy method of sketching is to use the Precise Input toolbar. As mentioned in Chapter 1, it allows precise XY positioning of a point, either with absolute values from the 0,0 origin point or relative (delta) distances from a previous point. You can display the toolbar by picking View/Toolbar/ Precise Input. If there's a checkmark beside the menu item, it is on (see Figure 2.10). The various buttons/tools must be "pressed in" to be active. The following describes the various tools.

	Relative Origin	Selects a point as a temporary origin. The point must be a valid point on the sketch. You turn on the button and then select a point. To turn it off, pick the button again.
	Relative Orientation	Not available in sketching. Used to rotate the axes.
	Delta Input	Sets the last point picked or entered as the reference point. The next value you enter will be relative to the last point. You have to pick or enter a starting point, then you can turn Delta Input on. To help you identify the last point, a temporary 3D Indicator appears at the last point entered.

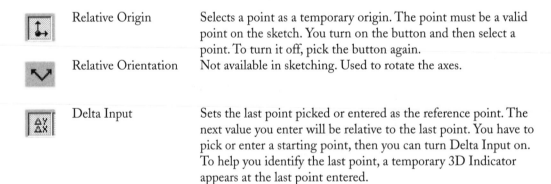

Figure 2.10   Precise Input toolbar

Context Menu

If you right-click while sketching, the sketching context menu appears. This menu contains some options to help you with your sketches, such as midpoint, center, and intersection snaps.

Input Type

Sets the format for coordinate input. There are four formats:
- xy   X and Y relative coordinates from the origin
- x°   X coordinate and angle from X axis
- y°   Y coordinate and angle from Y axis
- d°   A distance and angle from the positive X axis

Coordinate Input

Based on origin and type of input. You can enter numeric values, parameters, or expressions to specify the location.

Hands-On: Sketching

1. Start Autodesk Inventor.

2. Start a new part file by using the Standard [in].ipt template file.

3. Open the Documents Settings dialog box, accessed from the Tools pull-down menu. Check your settings to Figure 2.7.

4. Open the Application Options dialog box, accessed from the Tools pull-down menu. Check your settings to Figure 2.8. Note that the Snap to Grid box is checked (turned on).

5. Display the Precise Input toolbar and dock it at the bottom of the screen by dragging it into position. Refer to Figure 2.11 to make sure the same tools are active when you start to sketch. You won't have access to the Precise Input toolbar settings until you activate an element sketch tool.

6. Note that major grid lines (thicker gray lines) lie along every inch. You'll need to use the Zoom tool to widen the view so that at least two major grid lines are visible on either side of the X and Y axis lines (black) running through the center of the screen.

7. Refer to Figure 2.12 and draw the same sketch using the Line tool. The sketch is 4 inches long and 2 inches high. Start the lower-left corner at X: −2 and Y: −1. Enter the values in the coordinate entry box or pick the points on the screen. Watch the coordinate readout in the lower-right of the screen.

Slowly draw the lines clockwise around the parameter of the tee by using the cursor to pick the various points. Because Snap to Grid is turned on, you

Figure 2.11   Precise Input toolbar

Figure 2.12   Tee sketch

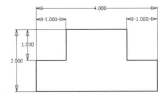

should be able to pick the locations easily. Watch closely as the implied constraints (such as vertical and perpendicular) appear as you near key locations.

When you have completed the perimeter, right-click and pick Done from the context menu.

8.   To save the part file, you have to "finish" the sketch. This will take you out of Sketch mode and put you into Feature mode. To do this, right-click with no command active. Pick Finish Sketch from the top of the context menu.

9.   Save your file as TEEPRO. Look at the browser. Note how the name of the part is now teepro.ipt. You've now had a taste of sketching. With the use of Implied constraints and Snap to Grid, the process is quite easy.

Geometric Constraints

Geometric constraints determine the orientation and relationship between sketch elements. Constraints that specify orientation to the coordinate system include fixed-point, horizontal, and vertical. Constraints that determine relationships between two elements include perpendicular, parallel, tangent, colinear, and concentric.

When you create a sketch, the sketch is analyzed and geometric constraints are added to suit the sketch. If a line is within approximately 5 screen pixels of being horizontal, it will be altered to be horizontal. The same thing applies to the other constraints. Because of this you must analyze your own design to determine how the sketch elements interrelate, then you can decide which geometric constraints are needed. You can delete constraints that have been automatically added but conflict with your design. You can also add your own constraints to solve a profile completely.

There are several methods for displaying constraints. You can display the constraints of a single element by activating the Show Constraints tool in the Sketch panel and then pausing over the element or picking the element. While the command is active, you can pick as many elements as you want. To display all the constraints, make sure no command is active, right-click, and pick Show All Constraints from the context menu. In both cases an Active Constraint box appears near the element (see Figure 2.13).

Figure 2.13   Active Constraint boxes for associated elements

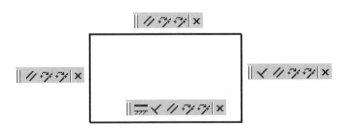

Active Constraint Box

The constraints that are applied to an element are contained with the Active Constraint box for each element. Each constraint applied is represented by a symbol.

Note the various symbols shown in Figure 2.13. You can see that a symbol may be repeated in a single Active Constraint box. In the rectangular sketch it is the coincident constraint that is repeated; it means that two elements (lines) share the same point, in this case endpoints.

To see which constraints apply to which elements, move the cursor over a constraint in an Active Constraint box. A red rectangle appears over the constraint symbol and the element or elements are highlighted in a reddish color. Points are shown with a yellow filled-in circle.

To delete a constraint, move the cursor over a constraint in an Active Constraint box and the red rectangle appears over the constraint symbol. Pick the symbol and the red rectangle turns blue. You can either press the Del key or right-click and pick Delete. When you delete a constraint for one element, you may find that constraints for other elements are deleted as well. Quite often many constraints in different elements are linked to each other.

To hide the Active Constraint boxes individually, pick the × in the box. To hide them all, make sure no command is active, right-click, and pick Hide All Constraints from the context menu.

When you create a sketch, the sketch is analyzed and geometric constraints are added to suit the sketch.

Adding Constraints

Even though geometric constraints are added automatically while you are sketching, they will not always constrain the sketch exactly the way you want them to. Sometimes you must delete particular constraints while adding others to make the sketch conform to your design.

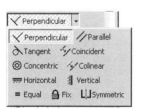

The Sketch Panel bar contains the tools to add geometric constraints to a sketch. The geometric constraints are contained in a flyout. If you pick the down arrow next to the constraint, the various geometric constraint tools are displayed.

Once you've picked a constraint to activate it, you can then pick an element to add constraints to it. Depending on the type of constraint, you may have to pick a second element to form a relationship with the first element. For instance, the perpendicular constraint requires two elements and the first element must be perpendicular to the second. A good idea is to display the constraints before adding others. This way you can see what is already constrained and what you need to delete or add. The method for deleting geometric constraints was explained in the preceding section.

Active Constraint Box Obscuring Geometry?

If the Active Constraint box obscures geometry, you can pick the vertical bar within the box and drag the box to a new location.

Figure 2.14
Geometric constraint
symbols

↙ Perpendicular	⟲ Coincident	═ Horizontal	⫿ Fix
// Parallel	◎ Concentric	⫻ Vertical	⟨Ɔ Symmetry
↘ Tangent	↖ Colinear	= Equal	

Fully Solved Profile

Always fully solve a profile with a combination of geometric and dimensional constraints. For a part to be truly parametric every piece of the profile should be fully solved. Leaving off a constraint allows the profile to wander, leading to unexpected results.

Geometric Constraint Context Menu

If you right-click with no command active, you can pick the Create Constraint flyout from the context menu. You then can pick the constraint you want to apply.

The following is an explanation of the different geometric constraints listed in the order that they appear in the geometric constraints flyout. Remember from previous material that geometric constraints determine the orientation and relationship between sketch elements. Constraints that specify orientation to the coordinate system include fixed-point (fix), horizontal, and vertical. Constraints that determine relationships between two elements include perpendicular, parallel, tangent, colinear, and concentric. The symbol for each geometric constraint is shown in Figure 2.14.

Perpendicular	Lines are forced to run 90° to each other.
Parallel	Lines are forced to be parallel to each other.
Tangent	A curve and a line are forced to be tangent to each other.
Coincident	Two points or a point and an element are forced to touch each other.
Concentric	Two arcs, circles, or ellipses are forced to use the same center point.
Colinear	Lines are forced to align along the same line.
Horizontal	Lines are forced to run parallel to the X axis.
Vertical	Lines are forced to run parallel to the Y axis.
Equal	One element is forced to have the same size as a second element.
Fix	Points or Elements are fixed in their relative position to the sketch coordinate system.
Symmetry	Lines, arcs, circles, ellipses, and spline segments are forced to become aligned symmetrically about a selected line.

Hands-On: Geometric Constraints

These exercises will give you exposure to adding constraints. The profiles you will be working on have already been created. The first one, TEEPRO, you created; the others came as part of the CD. If you followed Appendix A, they should have been copied to the c:\iainv subdirectory.

Displaying Constraints

1.   Open your TEEPRO file.

2.   Since you had to save the file in Part mode, it opens in Part mode. The view of the part/sketch may be an isometric one. This is a common way to display a part.

You need to switch to Sketch mode. To do this, double-click the Sketch1 heading in the browser. The entire sketch may turn red to signify it is active. It will return to normal when you pause your cursor on an element of the sketch.

3.   Right-click to bring up the context menu and select Show All Constraints from the menu. Remember no command should be active when you do this. To make sure no command is active, pick the Select button at the left end of the Command toolbar. Since the constraints were added automatically, most of them should be coincident and parallel, with a few perpendicular. Refer to Figure 2.14 and your screen to make sure you can easily identify the constraints in your sketch.

4.   To test your constraints, you're going to move some of the elements to see what happens.

Pick and drag on the top-most horizontal line of the sketch, upwards. Note how the vertical lines are connected to the horizontal line and stretch as you move. This is because the endpoints of the lines are coincident. Release the mouse button to stop dragging.

Pick and drag any corner of the sketch in any direction. Because of the perpendicular and parallel constraints, the lines/elements stay at right angles to each other. Release the mouse button to stop dragging.

The constraints that are applied to the sketch affect how it can be modified. When you try to move an element, you should be aware of what constraints have been applied. You may find that you have to delete a constraint to alter an element and then add it on again.

5.   Don't save the sketch, but you should close it by selecting the File/Close pull-down menu.

Adding Horizontal and Vertical Constraints: EX2B

This exercise will get you started adding constraints.

6.   Open file invex2B.ipt from the c:\iainv folder. Note that the file is in Part mode and in isometric view.

First, let's display the view perpendicular to the sketch. Highlight the label Sketch1 in the browser by picking it once. Note that the elements in Sketch1 turned blue in the graphics screen signifying that Sketch 1 is selected.

With the sketch highlighted, pick the Look At tool from the Standard toolbar. The view will rotate until the sketch is parallel with the screen. The profile on the screen should look similar to Figure 2.15. As you can see, the lines are all at different angles. You are going to add vertical and horizontal constraints to force them to follow the X and Y axes. Switch to sketch mode as you did with the TEEPRO sketch earlier.

7.   First, display the constraints using the Show All Constraints context menu item. Note how there are only coincident constraints at this point. Sometimes it can be easier to profile a sketch with no constraints. This is done by holding down on the Ctrl key when drawing a sketch element.

8.   Add the horizontal constraints first using the Horizontal tool. Pick the tool and pick the top almost horizontal line. Note how the profile moved when

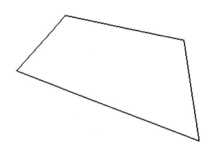

Figure 2.15   Profile to have geometric constraints applied

you added the constraint. This is perfectly normal. The profile will alter shape and position as more constraints are added. With the Horizontal Constraint command still active, pick the bottom almost horizontal line. Pick the Select tool or press the Esc key to exit the command. Your profile should now look similar to Figure 2.16(a).

9. Now use the Vertical Constraints tool and add vertical constraints to the two almost vertical lines. When done, your profile should look similar to Figure 2.16(b). You may have to pan down the screen or use the Zoom All tool to see all the geometry. You also may have to move the constraint bars so that they're easier to see. Did you notice how the geometry moved around the fixed point? Look at the constraints bar in the lower-left corner that contains a single constraint. You can add fixed constraints anywhere on the profile. It has the effect of locking the movement of the point you fixed.

10. Save the profile as EX2B.

11. If your TEEPRO profile did not have the proper horizontal and vertical constraints, open the file and add them as you did in the preceding steps.

Figure 2.16   Profile with (a) horizontal and (b) vertical constraints added

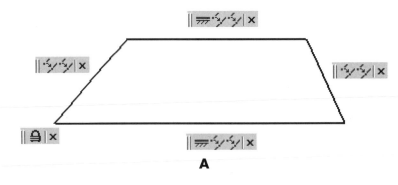

A

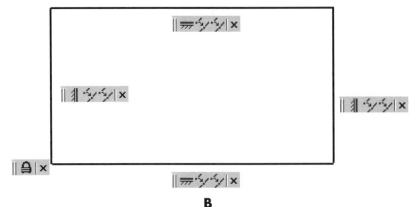

B

Adding Collinear, Tangent, and Concentric Constraints: EX2C

In this exercise, you're going to add collinear, tangent, and concentric constraints. Remember from the earlier list: the collinear constraint lines up two lines; tangent causes a line and an arc to become tangent; and concentric causes two arcs to share the same center.

12.   Open file invex2C.ipt from the c:\iainv folder. Note that the file is in Part mode and an isometric view.

As before, display the view perpendicular to the sketch and then switch to sketch mode. The profile on the screen should look similar to Figure 2.17.

13.   First display the constraints using the Show All Constraints context menu item. You'll have to move the constraint bars so that you can see them more clearly. To find out which bar goes with which element, pause your cursor over any constraint and observe what elements are highlighted. Identify the various constraints by referring back to Figure 2.14.

14.   The first step is to force the bottom horizontal lines to line up with each other. This is accomplished with the use of the Collinear Constraint tool. Pick the tool and first pick the left horizontal line 5 and then pick the other horizontal line 4. Note that the right line moved automatically to align with the left line. This is because the fixed point was at the corner of the left line. Press the Esc key twice to exit the command. Your profile should look similar to Figure 2.18(a).

15.   Now you're going to add some more tangent constraints to the arcs so that they blend smoothly with the vertical lines. Pick the Tangent Constraint tool and then pick the large arc and the vertical line on the far right. Note how the line moved over so that it's now tangent to the arc. Now pick the smaller arc and the vertical line on the inside left. The inside lines shifted so that they're tangent to the small arc. Your profile should look similar to Figure 2.18(b).

Figure 2.17   Profile showing preliminary geometric constraints

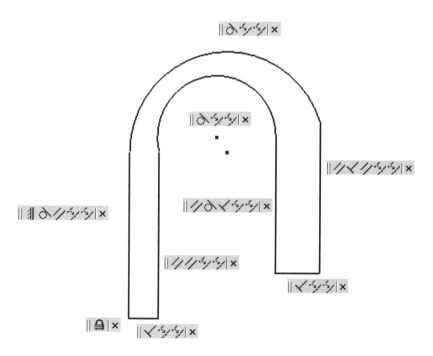

Figure 2.18 Profile
with collinear, tangent,
and concentric
constraints added

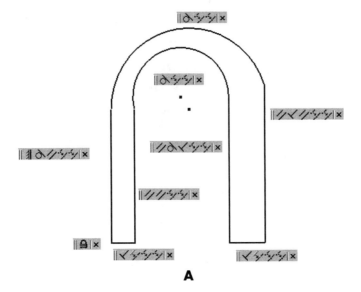

A

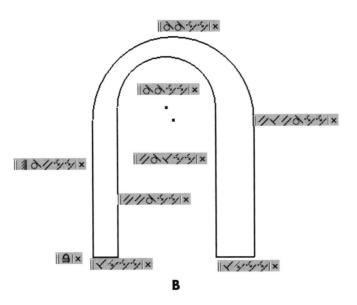

B

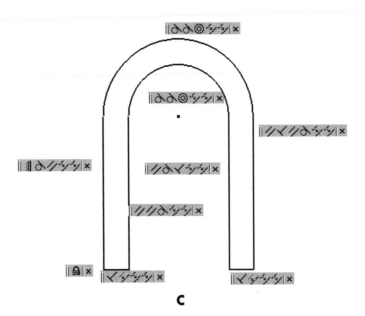

C

16. The last part of this exercise is to change the center of the smaller arc so that it matches that of the larger arc. This involves the use of the Concentric tool. Pick the tool, then pick the larger arc and then the smaller arc. The arc should now have the same centers as shown in Figure 2.18(c).

17. Save the profile as EX2C.

Adding Tangent and Radius Constraints: EX2D

In this exercise you will add some more tangent constraints and the equal constraint. The radius constraint is used to match the radii of two or more arcs or circles. In this way, if you change the radius of one arc or circle, the others will follow.

18. Open file invex2D.ipt from the c:\iainv folder. Note that the file is in Part mode and in isometric view.

As before, display the view perpendicular to the sketch and then switch to Sketch mode. The profile on the screen should look similar to Figure 2.19.

19. First display the constraints using the Show All Constraints context menu item. You'll have to move the constraint bars so that you can see them more clearly. Note how there are vertical, horizontal, perpendicular, and some tangent constraints. Also note that one of the arcs already has a dimensional constraint on it. This is important to do before applying radius constraints. In this way, you will control which one is used as the control arc.

How Do You Know the Order in Which to Constrain Certain Elements?

For most constraints it doesn't really matter which one you pick first. What does control how the elements move when a constraint is applied is the order in which you created the elements. In order, the second element moves towards the first and so on. The only thing that will override this is to apply a fixed constraint to stop an element or point from moving.

Figure 2.19 Profile to have geometric constraints applied

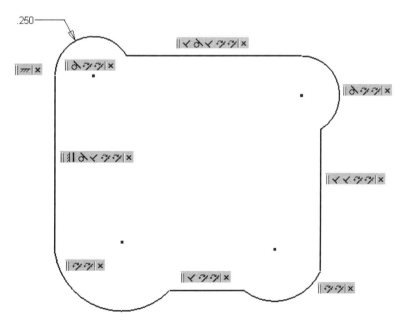

20. Now you're going to add some more tangent constraints to the arcs so that they blend smoothly with the vertical lines. Pick the Tangent Constraint tool and pick each arc and line that requires a tangent. There will be six pairs of lines and arcs. Your profile should look similar to Figure 2.20(a).

Note how many tangent constraints are in the figure. If your sketch does not match, add the constraints that are missing.

21. Pick the Equal Constraint tool and pick the arcs in the following order: pick the dimensioned arc and then one of the nondimensioned arcs; repeat for the three undimensioned arcs. The profile should appear as shown in Figure 2.20(b). All the radii now match arc 1 with a radius of 0.250.

22. Now to show the power of using the Equal constraint, you're going to change the radius dimensional constraint. Double-click on the dimension value. An Edit Dimension dialog box appears. Enter a value of 0.5 and see what happens. All the radii changed because of the Equal constraint.

Figure 2.20   Profile with tangent and equal constraints added

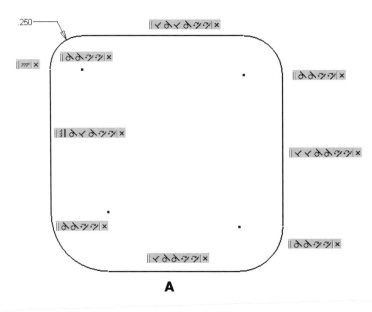

A

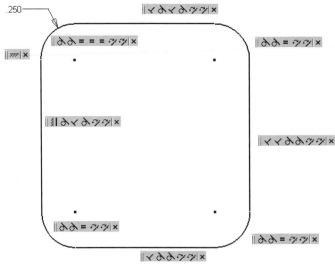

B

23. Save the profile as EX2D. You've now had some exposure to adding geometric constraints. The next step is to learn about dimensional constraints. Then you will see how easy it is to change the size of an object that has a dimensional constraint applied to it.

Dimensional Constraints

Dimensional constraints specify the length, radius, or rotation angle of the geometric elements in your sketch. Geometric constraints force the profile to conform to a specific shape; dimensional constraints, on the other hand, add the parametric characteristic to the profile. You can change a dimension at any time and its new value is immediately reflected in the design.

It is easy to change the size of an object that has a dimensional constraint applied to it.

Method of Entry and Display of Dimension Values

Dimensions can be shown and entered as either numeric constants or as equations. You can even use a combination on one profile (see Figure 2.21). Part (a) shows the profile with numeric dimensions and Part (b) shows it with equations. Using equations on the profile can add to its versatility because when you modify one dimension, a series of dimensions change in relation to it (see 2.21(b)). Note the formula d6 = d4/2. Whenever you change the dimension d4, dimension d6 will change to always be $^1/_2$ the value of d4. Using formulas, you can easily customize parts that have dimensions that are specifically related to each other. The rule of thumb for using numeric values versus equations is: Use numeric values when the size of an element is *not* related to another element and use an equation when the size of an element is directly related to another element.

You can enter an equation whenever you are asked to enter a dimension value. Usually it is easier to let the program first add a numeric value and then change the dimension value to an equation by double-clicking on a dimension value. A dialog box appears allowing you to enter a new value. You'll notice that the suffix to the value is the unit such as *in* for inches, *mm* for millimeters, and *ul* for unitless. You can enter a value in a different unit than you started the drawing in by including the unit suffix as in 30mm or 6in. When you're dividing a variable with a value, the value should be unitless (ul).

Figure 2.21 A profile showing dimensions as numeric values and equations

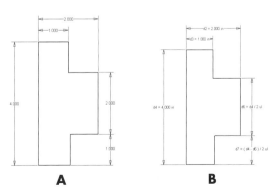

A   B

Entering Dimension Values

It is often best to enter dimensional values in decimal format. If you use fractions, you must enter them as an equation, such as 3 + 1/4, which equals 3.25. If you entered 3 − 1/4, it would translate as 2.75.

You should enter the most accurate values possible. Even though the numbers might be displayed with only two decimal places, Inventor retains up to six decimal places.

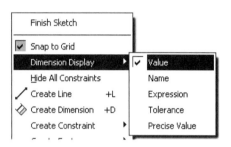

To change the display of the dimensions, right-click in open graphic space (with no command active) to bring up the context menu. Select Dimension Display to open the flyout. From the menu you can select Value, Name, Expression, Tolerance, or Precise Value.

Value	Displays the numeric value of the dimension.
Name	Displays the variable used to describe the dimension such as d3 or d5.
Expression	Displays the formula or expression for the dimension such as d2 = d3/2 ul.
Tolerance	Shows the dimension as a tolerance.
Precise Value	Shows the value with the maximum number of decimal points.

Dimension Order

You should usually dimension the larger elements first. This will help to keep the sketch from distorting during dimensioning. Remember that you're using a combination of geometric and dimensional constraints to solve the profile. You do not necessarily have to dimension every element in the profile. Some of the elements may be constrained by other elements. It is important to review the geometric constraints before dimensioning the element (see Figure 2.22). This profile requires only three dimensions because most of the geometry is controlled by geometric constraints. Review the various constraints in Figure 2.22. If you add too many geometric constraints, you may get the message that "Adding this constraint will overconstrain the sketch." The program will notify you if you

Dimension Styles

Dimensioning in Inventor is controlled by the dimension styles. These are set by the drawing standard used in the template that started the initial drawing. Under the Format pull-down menu, you'll find Standards, Dimensions Styles, and Text Styles. You can create your own styles and apply them in the Standards dialog box.

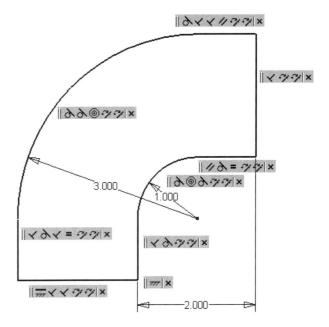

Figure 2.22 A dimensioned profile and its geometric constraints

try to add a dimension that will overconstrain or conflict with another previously placed dimension. The message is usually: "Adding this dimension will overconstrain the sketch. Do you want to create a Driven Dimension?" A driven dimension is a reference dimension shown in brackets as in [3.00]. It will be displayed but it cannot be edited because its value is driven by another dimension.

Dimensioning the larger elements first helps to keep the sketch from distorting during dimensioning.

Placing and Changing Dimensions

All the dimensions are created using a single command. It can be selected using the General Dimension tool from the Sketch Panel bar. The program knows when you pick on a line, arc, or circle and automatically snaps to the ends of lines and the centers of arcs or circles. *Note:* There is a tool called Auto Dimension. It will automatically apply geometric and dimensional constraints to the sketch. We suggest the beginner avoid this command until he or she is comfortable with Autodesk Inventor since there is a considerable loss of control over the type of dimensioning used.

When dimensioning a line, you can pick it and then place the dimension. The program automatically measures the line. If you're dimensioning between two different elements, simply pick near the end of each and the program automatically snaps to the endpoints.

When dimensioning a circle or an arc, pick along its circumference and then pick the location of the dimension. If you are dimensioning linearly, the extension line measures from the center of the arc or circle.

To dimension an angle, pick near the midpoint of each of the two lines and then pick the location of the dimension.

To change a dimension value, double-click on the dimensions value.

Moving Dimension Text

To alter the location of the dimension text, pause over the text until the Move cursor appears and then pick and drag. Remember that no other command can be active.

Hands-On: Adding Dimensional Constraints

In this exercise, you're going to add some dimensional constraints to your TEEPRO profile.

1.   Open your TEEPRO drawing. As before, display the view perpendicular to the sketch and then switch to Sketch mode. Display all the geometric constraints. They should look similar to Figure 2.23(a). If the constraints are different, correct your profile. You should notice that your profile is probably missing the collinear constraint on the two middle horizontal lines. This will make their heights match. Make sure you add it to your profile. Also, check to see where the Fixed point (fix) constraint is added. Look at Figure 2.23(a) and match yours to it. You may have to delete and add a new fixed point.

2.   Now add the necessary dimensions to your profile. Proceed to add the dimensions as shown in Figure 2.23(b). Your numeric values may not match the

Figure 2.23 Profile showing geometric and dimensional constraints

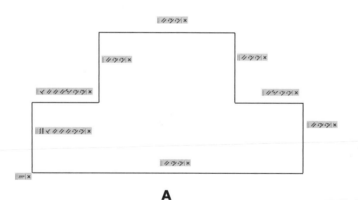

A

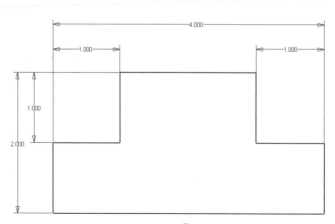

B

figure. Never fear. Remember the figure and your profile are both rough sketches.

3.   The next step is to change the dimension numeric values so that they will be more practical and conform to your initial design. You may skip entering new values if your values match Figure 2.21. However, you should practice editing the dimensions. Double-click the Overall Length dimension. When asked for the new dimension value, enter 4. Then, double-click the Overall Height dimension and enter a value of 2. Finally, double-click the other dimensions and enter values of 1.

4.   Save your drawing as TEEDIM before continuing.

5.   Experiment with changing the various dimensions, noting how the profile is affected. Now isn't that an easy way to alter a design—by simply changing the dimensions?

Note: Don't save the modified drawing.

Adding Equations

You are going to alter some of the dimensions in your profile to include equations so that you can see firsthand how they work. Figure 2.24(a) shows the dimension expressions displayed on the sketch.

6.   Open your TEEDIM drawing. As before, display the view perpendicular to the sketch and then switch to Sketch mode.

Figure 2.24 Sketch showing expressions before and after

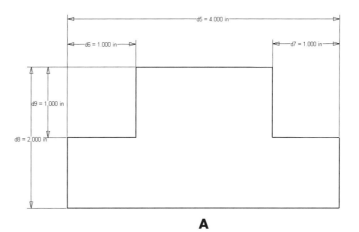

A

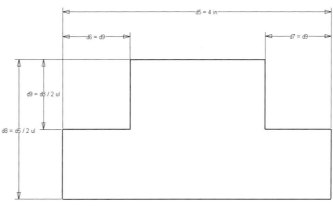

B

7. Right-click one of the dimension values and pick Show Expression from the context menu. Check what the identification is of the Overall Length dimension. It may be d5 as in our figure but it might be another number. Write down what it is.

8. Double-click the Overall Height dimension (it should have a value of 2). When asked what the new value is, enter the following equation: d5/2 (you may need to substitute the d5 with the identification from your dimension).

Note the identification of the Overall Height dimension. It may be d8. Now pick the second vertical dimension (it should have a value of 1) and enter the equation: d8/2 (you may need to substitute the d8 with the identification from your dimension).

Finally, change the two short horizontal dimensions so that they are equal to the short vertical dimension by entering the identification of the short vertical dimension (see Figure 2.22(b)). Remember to substitute the identifications in your sketch. You've now added four equations to your sketch that are all based on the overall length value. Your design should look similar to Figure 2.24(b). Let's test it out.

9. Double-click the Overall Length dimension. Change its value to 3 and see what happens. The two vertical dimensions changed as well. That's the power of using equations.

10. Save your drawing as TEEDIM.

11. Experiment with adding other equations to see what can be accomplished with such a simple design.

Editing a Sketch

In most cases you can highlight an element and drag it to change its location or size. If the element is constrained to another element, they'll both be affected. There's also a variety of tools to edit a sketch, whether it is in progress or complete. These are contained in the Sketch panel bar.

By using the editing tools, you can save yourself a lot of time later on because constraints that control the elements are placed automatically, depending on the tool used. A word of caution: When you modify an element that's already constrained, the results will be controlled by the existing constraints. This can affect the outcome. Sometimes you need to delete constraints to modify an element. The following are the editing tools as shown in the Sketch Panel bar:

Fillet/Chamfer	Adds a round or beveled corner to two intersecting elements.
Mirror	Creates a duplicate mirrored copy of selected elements. It requires a line element to mirror about.
Rectangular Array	Creates a series of related copies in two directions. To indicate the direction the copies are to travel, pick the arrow button and then pick an element on your sketch.
Circular Array	Creates a series of related copies around a point. To edit the pattern after it's created, right-click one of the elements and pick Edit Pattern from the context menu.
Offset	Creates a copy of an original element or elements to whatever distance you drag the cursor. You can dimension the offset distance afterwards. If you modify the original element or elements, the offset copy changes as well.

Adding Arcs to an Existing Profile

You will find it easier to use the FILLET command to add multiple arcs to your profile so that when it is re-solved, the radii will match.

Extend and Trim   Extends or trims an element to meet another existing element. Pick near the end of the element to extend or trim.

Move   Moves an element from one existing point to another existing point. If there's no existing point, you can create a temporary one using a point tool. Erase the point when complete.

Rotate   Rotates an element around an existing point using a specified angle.

Hands-On: Appending a Profile

In this exercise, you're going to add some more geometry to your TEEDIM profile and then use Append to update the profile with the new geometry.

1.   Open your TEEDIM drawing. As before, display the view perpendicular to the sketch and then switch to Sketch mode.

Right-click on a dimension value and pick Show Value from the context menu.

2.   Using the FILLET command, add two fillets as shown in Figure 2.25. The fillets should have a radius of 0.5.

3.   You may be wondering why only one dimension was needed when you added two arcs. When you used the FILLET command, Autodesk Inventor automatically applied the Tangent and equal geometric constraints. Once they were added, all that remained was to define the actual size of the radius by adding a dimension. Try changing the radius dimension to see what happens. Make sure you return the value to 0.50 before you save your drawing.

4.   Save your TEEDIM drawing.

Figure 2.25
Geometry added to the
TEEDIM profile

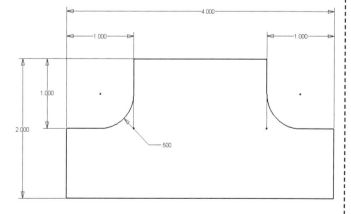

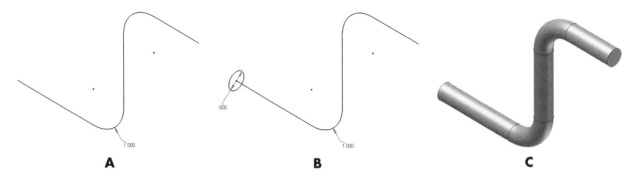

Figure 2.26   Using a path to create a part

Paths

This chapter deals mainly with closed profiles since you'll be using them most frequently. However, you can also create a path using the same sketch elements such as lines and arcs. A path can be an open loop or a closed loop. A path is used to sweep a profile along a particular route. You can practice creating and using paths later on when you're familiar with working in three dimensions. Paths can be two-dimensional (flat) or three-dimensional (such as a helix). Figures 2.26(a)–(c) show the three stages.

Stage 1   Draw a sketch of the desired path and complete the sketch by right-clicking and picking Finish Sketch from the context menu.

Stage 2   Draw a new sketch and turn it into a profile. The profile will be used as the outline.

Stage 3   The profile is swept along the path to create the three-dimensional part.

Sketch Doctor

There is a special tool to help you with problems with your sketches, aptly called the Sketch Doctor. To use it in Sketch mode, right-click with no command active. From the context menu, pick the Sketch Doctor menu item. A dialog box similar to Figure 2.27(a) appears. The first step is to pick the Diagnose Sketch button. A new dialog box appears listing the various problems to test for (see Figure 2.27(b)). The results of the test are then displayed. Picking the Next button examines and highlights where the problems are. Picking Next again goes into the treatment mode. Finally, picking Finish applies the treatment.

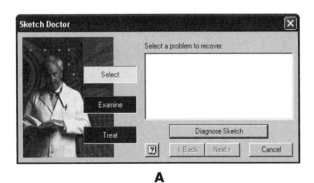

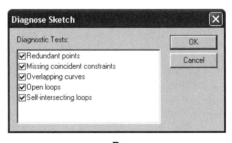

Figure 2.27   Sketch Doctor dialog box

In a Nutshell

The sketch is the basis of designing using Autodesk Inventor. The sketch can be used to create a profile, which in turn is used to create a three-dimensional part. The sketch can also be used to create a path used to sweep a profile. The profile shape and size are controlled by geometric and dimensional constraints.

You have now explored the steps to create a fully solved profile. You're now ready to move on to the next chapter and learn how to create a part from your profile.

 # Testing . . . testing . . . 1, 2, 3

Short Answers

    1. To create a sketch in Autodesk Inventor, begin by using _____ or _____ .

    2. The sketch used to generate a profile must be _____ .

    3. The two types of linetypes you can use in Inventor are _____ and _____ .

    4. The _____ dialog box controls units, 2D sketching, and 3D sketching.

    5. The three display modes are _____ , _____ , and _____ .

True or False

    6. Shapes used to form the outline of a sketch should overlap each other.   T or F

    7. The simpler the profile, the more complex it is to constrain.   T or F

    8. When you start sketching, implied constraints are inactive.   T or F

    9. Geometric constraints that are added automatically will always constrain the sketch the way you want to.   T or F

    10. You should try to dimension the larger elements first.   T or F

What?

    1. Explain the procedure to edit a sketch.

    2. What elements should you dimension first? Why?

    3. List and explain the difference between geometric and dimensional constraints.

4. Is it better to take time drawing your sketch accurately or to use that time to perfect the finished product? Support your answer clearly.

5. What's the most important rule for a beginner user of Inventor? Why?

6. Describe the procedure to get from a blank piece of paper to a profile.

Let's Get Busy!

Some of the assignments at the end of each chapter will be used in later assignments so
that you can build on what you have learned and practiced. These types of assignments
will be marked with a building block symbol as shown in the margin next to this text.
Whenever you see this symbol, you can be certain that the file created will be used later
on in another assignment.

1. Draw the sketch shown in Figure 2.28, profile it, and check that the geometric
   constraints match Part (b). Add any missing constraints and delete those that are
   not necessary. Once the geometric constraints are added, add the dimensions.
   Save your profile as SK2A.

2. Draw the sketch shown in Figure 2.29(a), and use the Offset tool to copy the
   large arc, the two small vertical lines tangent to the arc, and the two horizontal
   lines an approximate distance of 0.5. Do *not* pick the larger vertical lines. If you
   do, the offset will not work. You'll then need to add some coincident, colinear,
   and equal constraints. Add the dimensions shown in Part (b). Display the dimensions as equations and edit the dimensions by changing some of them to equations (refer to Part (b)). Once this is done, try changing some of the numeric values to see what happens. Add more equations as you desire. Save your profile as
   SK2B.

3. Draw the sketch shown in Figure 2.30(a), profile it, and check that the geometric
   constraints match Part (b). Add any missing constraints and delete those that are
   not necessary. Add the dimensions shown in Part (b). Display the dimensions as
   equations and edit the dimensions by changing some of them to equations (refer
   to Part (c)). Once this is done, try changing some of the numeric values to see
   what happens. Add more equations as you desire. Save your profile as SK2C.

4. Draw the sketch shown in Figure 2.31(a), profile it, and check that the geometric
   constraints match Part (b). Add any missing constraints and delete those that are
   not necessary. Add the dimensions shown in Part (a). Display the dimensions as
   equations and edit the dimensions by changing some of them to equations (refer
   to Part (b)). Once this is done, try changing some of the numeric values to see
   what happens. Add more equations as you desire. Save your profile as SK2D.

Figure 2.28 Parallel
Wedge—Sketch 2A

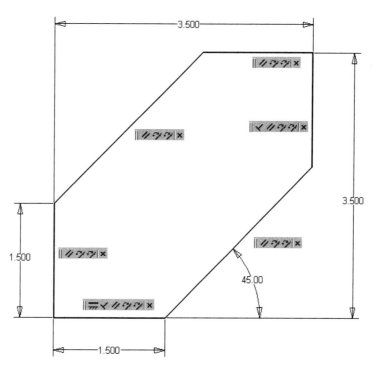

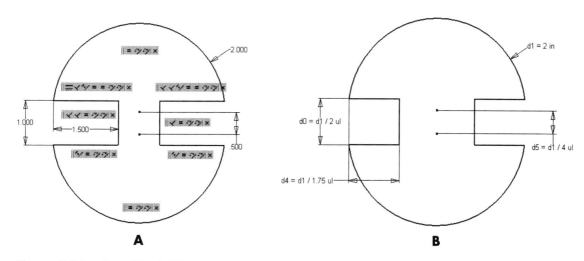

A

B

Figure 2.29 Key—Sketch 2B

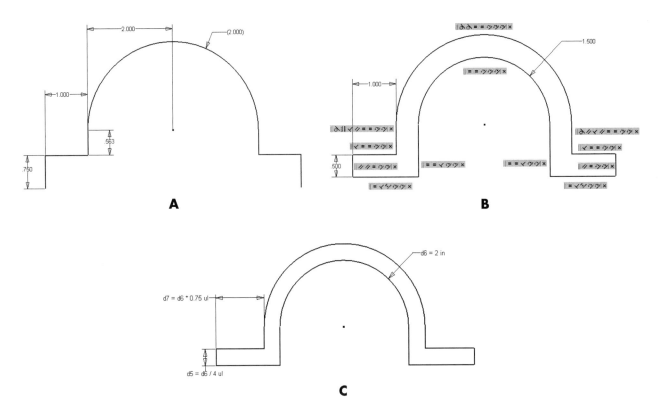

Figure 2.30   Collar Clamp—Sketch 2C

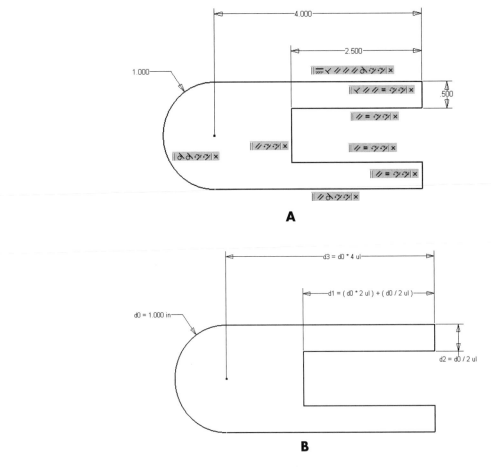

Figure 2.31   Pivot Joint—Sketch 2D

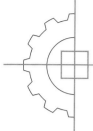

Chapter 3

Part Creation

Key Concepts

- ◆ Coordinate Systems
- ◆ Planar Creation and the UCS Icon
- ◆ Shade Modes and 3D Model Viewing
- ◆ Sketch Features
- ◆ Extrude, Revolve, and Sweep

What Is a Part?

A part is a three-dimensional solid object composed of various features that define its shape and size. As the design of the part evolves it can contain a variety of features such as fillets, holes, and a shell. But to start you have to create your first basic part. This involves your initial, or base, profile. Creating the starting part feature involves such actions as extruding, revolving, and sweeping profiles. Though they are used as the starting point, they can also be used over and over again to create very complex parts.

This chapter introduces you to three-dimensional concepts and moves into actual part creation making use of three different processes: extrude, revolve, and sweep. After you're able to create using these methods, you'll be introduced to more advanced concepts relating to working in 3D. These involve viewing the 3D model in different ways and the creation of working surfaces to allow you to create on any axis. These will be covered in the next chapter.

Introduction to 3D

To move from your two-dimensional sketches and profiles to a three-dimensional part, you need to understand some 3D concepts. This section reviews the basic concepts so that you will be able to understand the Autodesk Inventor creation process more easily.

The base part is used as the starting point and can also be used over and over again to create very complex parts.

The mental skills required to work in 3D are different from those needed for drawing in 2D. In drafting (2D), the user translates the three-dimensional attributes of an object into flat, two-dimensional views—top, front, and side as shown in Figure 3.1.

In modeling (3D), all three dimensions are taken into consideration. This sounds complicated, but actually it allows the design to be formulated faster because the user can see the entire model at any time, instead of having to work on one 2D view at a time.

Figure 3.1
Transforming a 3D object into a 2D drawing

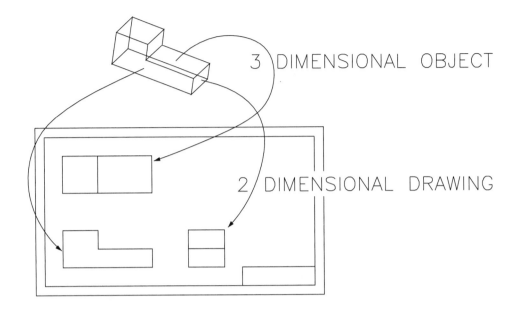

When creating your sketches, you're basically working in 2D, using the X and Y axes. In the creation of a part, a third axis is added: the Z axis. Figures 3.2(a) and (b) show the two-dimensional profile and the three-dimensional part.

Coordinate Systems

To keep track of the three axes, there are two coordinate systems in Autodesk Inventor: the model coordinate system and the sketch coordinate system. For ease of reference we will refer to them as MCS and SCS.

The MCS is Autodesk Inventor's master coordinate system. It has X, Y, and Z coordinates with origin points of 0x, 0y, and 0z. However, you can't change the orientation of this system or move it in any way. This guarantees that you cannot get "lost" in 3D space. The WCS can always be used as a frame of reference. It always stays right where you last saw it! The 3D Indicator shows you the orientation of the MCS.

Whenever you sketch, it takes place on the SCS with its own X,Y,Z axes. When you start a new part, the sketch coordinate systems is aligned with the model coordinate system, MCS. Although the MCS can't be moved, the SCS can be. Moving the SCS is necessary when you start working on a three-dimensional part. More details will be provided about moving the SCS in Chapter 4. You will use the SCS to create planes on which you create your geometry. Figure 3.3 shows a hand holding a cube. If that were your hand

Figure 3.2
(a) Turning a two-dimensional profile into a (b) three-dimensional part

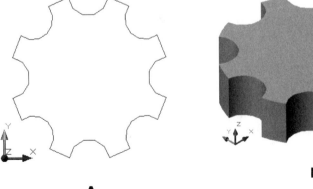

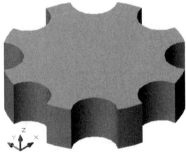

A

B

Figure 3.3
Manually drawing on
the face of a cube

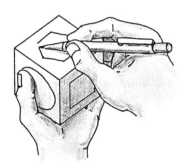

holding the cube, and you wanted to draw on it with a pencil, all you would need to do is pick the side to draw on, get a pencil, and proceed to draw. The procedure is similar in Autodesk Inventor. You must tell the program on which plane (side) the drawing or construction is going to take place. The Sketch plane can be thought of as a transparent sheet of paper that extends to infinity in all directions. Once the plane is defined, you can draw anywhere on it.

After you have created some simple parts using the default Sketch plane, you will learn how to move your SCS around to work on any surface or plane.

Planar Creation

When you perform any construction in three dimensions, it is still based on a flat, 2D plane (planar). A plane is defined by its XY coordinates. The direction is defined by the Z axis. When you start a new part, it's automatically in Sketch mode and the XY plane is parallel to the screen and the positive portion of the Z axis is pointing toward you.

The Sketch plane should be thought of as a transparent sheet of paper that extends to infinity in all directions.

To help you visualize the three axes, use the right-hand rule. This rule is illustrated in Figure 3.4. To try it yourself, hold your right hand in front of the screen with the back of the hand parallel to the screen, and make a fist. Now extend the thumb out, toward the right; this points in the positive X direction. Extend the index (or first) finger upward; this points in the positive Y direction. And, finally, extend the middle finger towards yourself; this points in the positive Z direction. If you rotate your hand in any direction, the orientation of the axes to each other remains the same. When you move your SCS around on your model, the orientation of the X, Y, and Z axes remains the same.

Figure 3.4   The right-hand rule for axis orientation

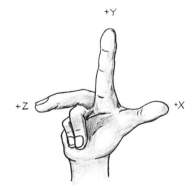

3D Indicator and Coordinate System Indicator

You have probably noticed the 3D Indicator at the bottom-left corner of the graphics screen. It's used to show you the MCS XYZ axes and is helpful when viewing the part in 3D. You can tell if you're above, below, left, right, in front, or behind just by following the orientation of the axis arrows. As mentioned in Chapter 1, the green indicator line lies on the Y axis and the arrowhead points in a positive direction, the red indicator line lies on the Y axis pointing in a positive direction, and the blue indicator line lies on the Z axis pointing again in a positive direction.

To display or hide the 3D Indicator, pick the Tools/Applications Options pull-down menu item. The Options dialog box appears. Under the General tab there is a Show 3D Indicator box. If it's checked, the 3D Indicator is turned on (visible).

There's also a coordinate system indicator for the SCS. To display or hide the SCS coordinate system indicator, pick the Tools/Applications Options pull-down menu item. Under the Sketch tab there is a Coordinate System Indicator box (Figure 3.5). If it is checked the SCS coordinate system indicator is turned on (visible).

The 3D Indicator icon is used as a directional beacon as you work on your sketch. When you move the SCS, the icon changes to reflect the move. Even though you can turn the icon off, we recommend that you keep it visible so you don't get disorientated. As well, it should be set on the origin point.

Once you've identified the plane you'll be working on, the SCS coordinate system indicator re-orients itself to help you identify the sketching or working surface. The intersection of the three axis lines indicates the 0,0,0 origin of the sketch plane. Figure 3.6(a) shows a part with the 3D Indicator visible; Figure 3.6(b) shows the same part with the addition of the SCS coordinate system indicator. It's hard to tell in a black and white image but the XYZ axes of the SCS and the MCS are different.

Figure 3.5
Options/Sketch dialog box showing Coordinate System Indicator box

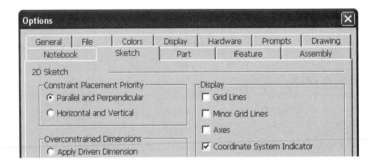

Figure 3.6 (a) 3D Indicator and (b) addition of Coordinate Indicator

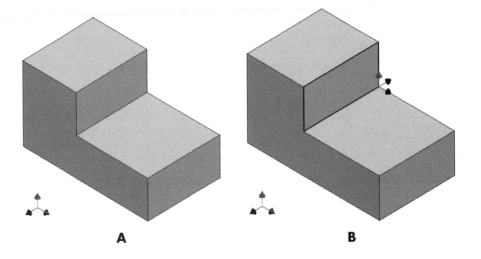

A   B

When you create or re-activate a sketch plane, the SCS coordinate system is active as well. This is why it's a good idea that you have the SCS coordinate system indicator visible so that you know the exact orientation of the active XYZ axes for creation purposes.

Display Modes

There are three different display modes to display your part: wireframe, hidden edge, and shaded. Wireframe allows you to see through the part so that all the edges are visible. This is extremely useful during construction, especially when you need to pick edges or snap to corners. Shade mode, on the other hand, applies color to the surfaces of the part. In this way, the part appears more tangible. This is useful when you are viewing the part to see if it is the correct shape. Hidden edge is a combination of the two. The part is shaded but the lines that would normally be hidden are also shown. Figure 3.7 shows the three display modes. You can switch modes using the Display tool flyout on the Standard toolbar.

3D Model Viewing

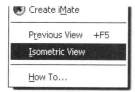

Because you're working in three dimensions, you need to be able to move around and view the model in three dimensions. There are a number of ways to do this, the simplest being the use of the right-click context menu and selecting the Isometric View menu item.

When you Select Isometric View, the view part slowly rotates until you're looking at the right-front-top isometric view. Figure 3.8 shows the isometric view. Compare it to Figure 3.7 which is not an isometric view.

As you work on your model, you'll find yourself wanting to see different views of the part. There are other methods, such as rotate, look at, and camera, which will be

What Display Mode to Use?

You'll find that you'll switch back and forth between shaded and wireframe. With wireframe it is much easier to see edges, allowing you to pick them as needed. Shaded is more useful when you want to check the part's current appearance.

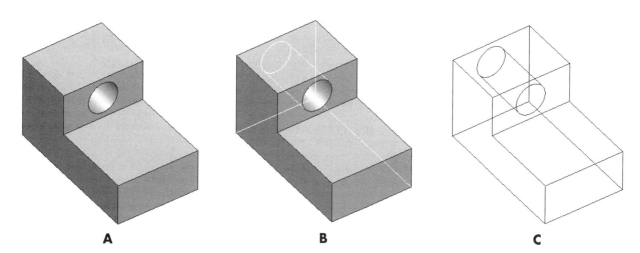

Figure 3.7 Display modes: (a) shaded, (b) hidden edge, and (c) wireframe

Figure 3.8   Isometric
view

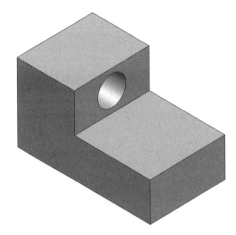

explained later in the next chapter. We have explained just enough here so that you can start creating your parts as soon as possible.

Sketch Features

A sketch feature is a three-dimensional solid generated with a sketch. There are six methods for creating a sketch feature: extrude, revolve, sweep, loft, rib, and coil. This chapter will discuss the first three. The other three are more advanced methods.

You can build on an existing part by adding another profile and generating a sketch feature. The feature can either join to the existing part or cut away from it. In this way, by using sketch features you can create complex parts. To create sketches around your part involves creating sketch planes. This will be explained after you have learned how to create basic parts.

Extrude

The first and simplest method to create a sketch feature from your profile is to extrude the profile. Basically, the command takes your profile and extrudes it along the Z axis to create the three-dimensional shape. Figures 3.9(a) and (b) show a profile of a support yoke extruded into a part.

**There are six methods for creating a sketch feature:
extrude, revolve, sweep, loft, rib, and coil.**

When you select the Extrude tool you'll be presented with a dialog box similar to Figure 3.10. This dialog box is used to set the various design characteristics of the extru-

Figure 3.9   Profile of a support yoke extruded into a part

Figure 3.10 Extrude
dialog box

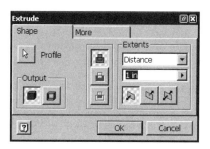

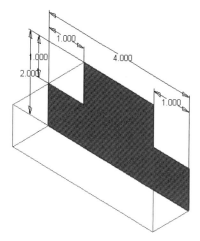

sion. Once you have entered the desired settings, pick the OK button and the extrusion of the part will appear on the screen. As you adjust settings in the dialog box, they'll be shown on the profile. The selected profile is shaded in solid blue and the extrusion is shown in green wireframe. *Note:* You can select more than one profile as long as they're part of the same sketch.

The following is an explanation of the various areas contained within the dialog box.

Shape	This area allows you to select the profiles to be used in the extrusion and to set the output (solid or surface).
Operation	This area is not labeled but contains various buttons that control how the extrusion is applied. There are three buttons stacked vertically: Join, Cut, and Intersect. If it's the first feature of the part, only the Join button is available.
More	Under the More tab you'll find a Taper value box. This allows you to taper the extrusion. A positive value tapers out and negative value tapers in.

The Join option is used to add a material, in the form of the extrusion, to the part.

The Cut option is used to remove material, in the form of the extrusion, from the part.

The Intersect option creates a new feature using the intersecting volume of the existing part and the extruded solid.

Extents   The Extents area is used to determine how the extrusion will be ended. There are five options: Distance, To Next, To, From–To, and All.

The Distance option extrudes the profile by a distance that you provide. You can enter distances in a variety of ways by picking on the down-arrow on the right of the distance value box.

The To Next option extrudes the profile to the next possible face or plane that you select.

The To option extrudes the profile to a face or plane that you select.

The From–To option extrudes the profile from beginning and ending faces or planes that you select.

The All option extrudes the profile through all features and sketches in the specified direction. The Join operation does not function with this option.

There are also three buttons that control the direction of the extrusion: positive Z, negative Z, and halfway in-between.

Displaying an Isometric View

Whenever you're generating sketch features such as extrusions, you show the display in an isometric view for two reasons: (1) this is the only way you will be able to see the directional arrow that tells you which way the part will be created and (2) you can see the part better as it is created.

Hands-On: Creating a Part Using Extrusion

In this Hands-On you're going to create an extrusion from your TEEDIM profile. As well, you will practice performing extrusions on exercise files.

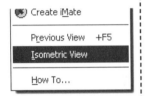

1. Open your TEEDIM profile.

2. You will need to display an isometric view of the profile so that you can see the direction on the extrusion. When you open a part file, it usually displays the part as an isometric view. If for some reason it's not displaying an isometric view, right-click in the graphics screen (with no command active). Select Isometric View from the context menu. Your screen should look similar to Figure 3.11(a). You may have to zoom out a bit to see all the dimensions.

3. Since there is only one profile, it will already be activated. Now pick the Extrusion tool and you should be presented with a dialog box similar to Figure

Sketch Features and Profile Dimensions

When you're entering values for sketch features such as the distance for extrusion, you can pick dimensional values straight from the profile. This applies the variable for the profile dimension to the extrusion distance. Later on, if you modify the selected profile dimension, the extrusion distance changes as well.

Figure 3.11
TEEDIM profile extruded into a part

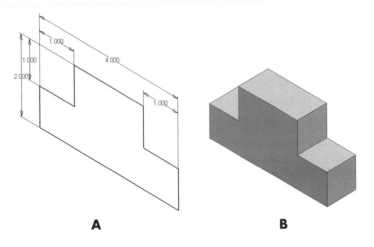

A   B

3.10. Look at your profile; there should be a green shade area that represents the profile to be extruded and a green wireframe shape that represents the extrusion.

Match your settings to Figure 3.10 and pick the OK button. Your profile should now have been extruded to look like Figure 3.11(b). It is now a three-dimensional part. If your part is not fully displayed, use ZOOM Extents to see it.

5.   Let's look at it in various display modes. Usually, by default, the part's displayed shaded. Change it to wireframe display. Now you can see the edges at the back of the part. This can be useful for relating various surfaces to each other. Unfortunately it's hard to see all the edges in an isometric view. How to remedy this will be explained in the next chapter. For now, change the Display mode to Hidden edge. This has the added feature of seeing the edges while still in Shade mode. You'll find yourself switching to different modes throughout your creation.

6.   Save a copy of your newly formed part as TEEEXT. Close the TEEPRO file without saving the changes.

Practice Using the Extrude Options: EX3A

1.   Open file invex3A.iam. It's an assembly file that contains two sketches. We've used an assembly file so that two sketches could be shown at one time. If they aren't displayed in an isometric view, change it to isometric.

2.   Right-click on invex3p1.ipt in the browser. This is the part file for the first sketch. A context menu appears. Select Edit from the menu. You'll notice that all the other items, except for the invex3p1 features, are "grayed-out." This is to help indicate which part you're working on in an assembly.

You should also note that the Features panel has appeared. Select the Extrude tool and match your settings to the dialog box shown in Figure 3.12. Note the direction buttons below the distance value. The button on the left is depressed, signifying the extrusion is in the positive Z direction. Pick the OK button when you're ready. The extruded sketch feature should now be created. Right-click and select Finish Edit.

Use the Zoom tool to zoom out a little to see both objects entirely.

3.   Right-click on invex3p2.ipt in the browser. This is the part file for the second sketch. As before, a context menu appears. Select Edit from the menu. You'll notice that the first extruded part is "grayed-out." This is to help indicate which part you're working on in an assembly.

Select the Extrude tool and match your settings to the dialog box shown in Figure 3.13. This time make sure that the direction button on the right is depressed, signifying the extrusion will be from the midplane and be half in the positive Z direction and half in the negative Z direction. Pick the OK button

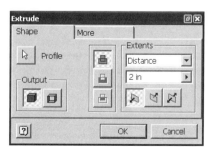

Figure 3.12   Extrude dialog box settings for invex3p1.ipt (part 1)

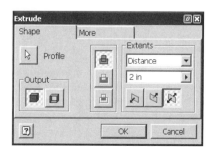

Figure 3.13   Extrude dialog box settings for invex3p2.ipt (part 2)

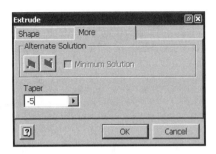
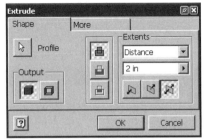

Figure 3.14   Extrude dialog box
settings with taper angle

Figure 3.15   Extrude dialog box
settings for invex3p2.ipt with taper angle

when you're ready. The extruded sketch feature should now be created. Compare
the two extrusions. Right-click and pick Finish Edit. Both extruded parts should
have the same color.

4.   Save a copy of the assembly file as EX3A1. Close the original file without saving the changes.

Using a Taper Angle

5.   Open the assembly file invex3A.iam again so that you have only the
two profiles on the screen.

6.   Highlight invex3p1.ipt as before and activate the EXTRUSION command. Match the settings to Figure 3.14. Note the addition of the Taper angle
value. This will cause the sides of the extrusion to be tapered. OK the box and see
the results. Your new part should have sloped sides. A negative taper angle slopes
inward, a positive taper angle slopes outward. Right-click and select Finish Edit.

7.   Highlight invex3p2.ipt and activate the EXTRUSION command.
Match the settings shown in Figure 3.15. This time you're using the midplane
button and a −5 taper angle. OK the box to see the results. The taper is now
broken into two directions, or midplane. These are some of the reasons for using
the midplane button.

8.   Save a copy of the assembly file as EX3A2. Close the original file without saving the changes.

9.   Open the assembly file invex3A.iam again and experiment with the different Extrude options. Try using the negative Z direction button to see what happens.

Revolve

The next method for creating a sketch feature from your profile is to revolve that profile
around an axis. The axis can be a line on the profile, or offset from the profile using a
construction line. Figures 3.16(a) and (b) show a pulley created through revolution. Note
the thin line below the profile in Figure 3.16(a). This is a construction line used as the
axis on which to rotate the profile. This has the effect of creating a hole in the final
revolved part (Figure 3.16(b)).

When you select the Revolve tool, the Revolve dialog box appears, similar to the one
shown in Figure 3.17. If there's only one profile sketch, it will be highlighted and the
Axis button will be depressed, prompting you to pick an axis on the sketch. As mentioned
before, you can pick an edge of the sketch, or a line offset from the sketch such as a con-

Figure 3.16 Pulley created from (a) a profile through (b) revolution

A

B

Figure 3.17 Revolve dialog box

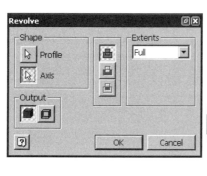

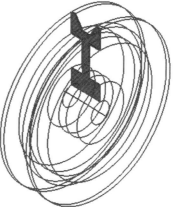

struction line. Once you've identified the axis, a green wireframe revolved shape appears showing how the part may be formed. You can make adjustments to the settings and then pick OK to apply them.

Shape   This area allows you to select the profiles to be used in the extrusion and to set the output (solid or surface).

Operation   This area is not labeled but contains various buttons that control how the extrusion is applied. There are three buttons stacked vertically: Join, Cut, and Intersect. If it's the first feature of the part, only the Join button is available.

Extents   This area sets the included angle of the revolution. Full is a complete 360°, while the Angle setting allows you to enter any angle.

Hands-On: Creating a Part Using Revolve

In this exercise, you're going to create a revolved feature from your TEEDIM profile. As well, you will practice performing revolutions on exercise files.

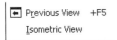

1.   Open your TEEDIM profile.

2.   Using the right-click context menu, display an isometric view of the profile. You may need to use the Zoom tool to reduce the view of the profile in order to make it easier to perform the revolve function (see Figure 3.18(a)).

3.   Since there's only one profile, it will already be activated. Now pick the Revolve tool. A dialog box similar to Figure 3.19 should be presented. Note that the Axis button is depressed. You're being prompted to pick an axis to revolve the profile around. Pick the long line on the bottom/base of the profile. As you move your cursor near the line to select, it is highlighted red. When you pick it, a green wireframe revolved shape appears.

Match your settings to Figure 3.19 by setting the Extents to Angle and change the angle to 180°. Observe your profile. It now shows a revolved path of 180°. Pick the OK button. Your profile should now have been revolved to look like Figure 3.18(b). It is now a three-dimensional part. If your part is not fully displayed, use ZOOM to see it.

4.   Save a copy of your newly formed part as TEEREV. Pick the Undo tool to revert the part back to its original profile.

Adding a Construction Axis Line

In this part of the exercise, you're going to create a construction line that is offset from the profile. This line will be used as the axis line for a new revolved part.

Figure 3.18
Revolved TEEDIM profile into a part

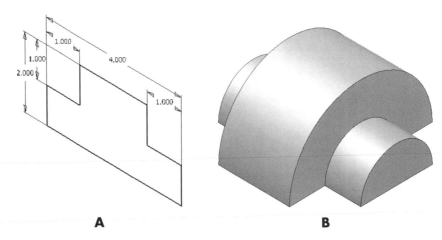

A   **B**

Figure 3.19
Revolve dialog box settings

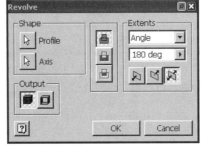
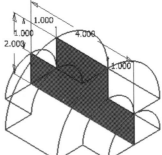

Construction
Normal
Construction

5. Make sure that your original TEEDIM is on the screen. Select the Sketch1 label in Browser to highlight the profile blue in the graphics screen. Pick the Look At tool to display a flat view of the profile.

6. Double-click on the Sketch1 label in Browser to switch to Sketch mode.

7. Change the Style box to read Construction instead of Normal. This box is found on the Standard toolbar at the top of the screen.

8. Make sure that the Inventor Precise Input toolbar is visible. Right-click on any toolbar and see if there is a checkmark next to the toolbar name.

9. Pick the Line tool and then pick the Precise Relative tool located at the left end of the Precise Input toolbar to make sure it is depressed.

The cursor now has a plus sign beside it, signifying that you're to pick a location for the temporary origin for the precise input. Move your cursor to the lower-left corner of the tee profile and pick the corner intersection. Note the coordinate icon appearing at the corner. Any input values you enter now will be based on this origin point.

Enter the start coordinates of X: −1, Y: −1 and end coordinates of X: 5, Y: −1 in the Precise Input toolbar. Right-click and enter Done. A brown line should appear similar to Figure 3.20. This is the construction line.

10. Use the General Dimension tool to add a dimension from the edge of the profile to the end of the construction line (see Figure 3.20).

11. Right-click and select Finish Sketch from the context menu.

12. Display an isometric view of the profile. Reduce the magnification so that you can see all the dimensions and the construction line.

13. Pick the Revolve tool and pick the construction line as the axis line. Revolve the profile to fill extents. Use the Zoom All tool to see the entire part.

Note how it has a hole in the middle because of the offset axis line.

14. Right-click on the Revolution1 label in Browser. Select Show Dimensions from the context menu. The sketch dimensions should now be shown on the part.

15. Double-click on the 1-inch dimension for the construction line offset. Enter 2 in the presented dialog box and pick the checkmark symbol to apply the dimension. The part has not changed yet.

16. Pick the Update tool to apply the change. The hole is now larger because of the increased value of the offset construction line. Now can you see the power of parametric dimensioning to modify designs?

Delete
Show Dimensions
Edit Sketch
Edit Feature

Update

Figure 3.20
Addition of
Construction line

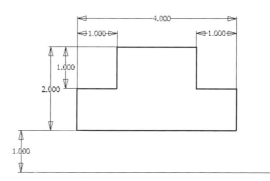

Sweep

The Sweep method for sketch feature creation involves both a profile and a path. The profile is extruded along the path, following the contours of the path to arrive at the final shape. The section on paths at the end of Chapter 2 gave you some exposure to this method. Figures 3.21(a) and (b) show the profile, a 3D pipe path, and the final section of pipe created through sweeping.

You need to draw a path and a profile sketch before you can use the command. The procedure to create sketch planes is explained in Chapter 4. The creation of the path can be a 2D sketch or a 3D sketch. If you need to create a 3D sketch, you must first create 3D sketch work points to establish where the 3D sketch geometric will travel. The creation of work points is explained later in Chapter 4. The Hands-On in this section has the profiles and paths already created so that you can experiment at this point of your learning. When using Sweep, a dialog box similar to Figure 3.22 will appear. This dialog box is used to set the various design characteristics of the sweep. Once you have entered the desired settings, pick the OK button and the sweep of the feature will appear on the screen.

The following is an explanation of the various areas contained in the dialog box.

Shape   This area allows you to select the profile and path to be used in the sweep
              and to set the output (solid or surface).

Operation   This area is not labeled but contains various buttons that control how the
              extrusion is applied. There are three buttons stacked vertically: Join, Cut,

Figure 3.21   A profile swept along a 3D pipe path to create the final section of pipe

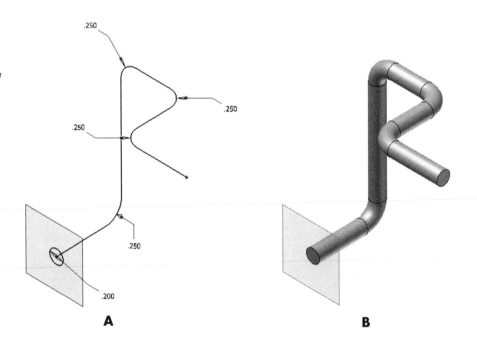

A   B

Figure 3.22   Sweep dialog box

and Intersect. If it's the first feature of the part, only the Join button is available.

More   This tab gives you access to adding a taper angle to the sweep. This will be demonstrated in the following exercise.

Hands-On: Creating a Part Using Sweep

In this Hands-On, you'll use a path and a profile that has already been created. The path and profile are used to create a part using the Sweep sketch feature.

1.   Open the part file invex3b.ipt. It contains a circle 2D sketch profile and a 2D sketch path. Your screen should be similar to Figure 3.23.

2.   Select the Sweep tool. You'll be presented with a dialog box similar to Figure 3.24(a). With the Path button depressed, pick the snake-shaped path. Match your dialog box settings to the figure and pick the OK button. A convoluted, snake-shaped part should now be displayed on your screen (see Figure 3.24(b)).

3.   Save a copy of your new part file as Snake1.

Figure 3.23   A circle profile and a path

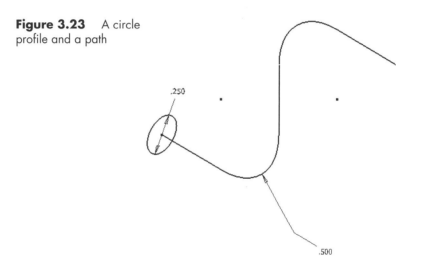

Figure 3.24   (a) The Sweep dialog box and (b) the results

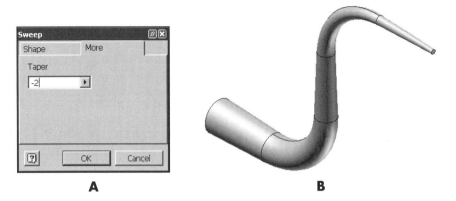

Figure 3.25   (a) The addition of a negative taper angle and (b) the results

Edit Feature

You're now going to edit the feature to cause it to taper.

4.   Right-click on the Sweep1 name in Browser and select Edit Feature from the context menu. You will be presented with the Sweep dialog box again. Pick the More tab and change the taper angle from 0° to −2°. This will cause the profile to taper in by 2° from the start to the end of the sweep (see Figure 3.25(a)).

Your sweep feature should now look similar to Figure 3.25(b).

5.   Save a copy of your edited part as Snake2.

In a Nutshell

Creation in 3D involves the three axes: X, Y, and Z. To keep track of these axes, there are two coordinate systems, the WCS, which never moves, and the SCS, which you can move to any orientation. The 3D Indicator shows you the orientation of the MCS. The Coordinate System Indicator assists you by giving you a visual guide to the orientation of the SCS. You can easily view the 3D model in isometric, displaying it in wireframe for construction, and shaded to check its progress more tangibly.

The starting point to part creation is the base profile. From this profile you can create a three-dimensional part using sketch features. A sketch feature is a three-dimensional solid created by such actions as extrude, revolve, and sweep. These features can be added (joined) or subtracted (cut) from an existing part.

Now that you have had a taste of creating in three-dimensions, let's go into more detail in the areas of viewing the model in 3D and creating sketch planes, topics covered in the upcoming Chapter 4.

Testing . . . testing . . . 1, 2, 3

Short Answer

1. The _____ is a fixed coordinate system while the _____ can be re-oriented.

2. To begin the creation process in Autodesk Inventor, you start with a(n) _____ and then you alter it through processes such as those covered in Chapter 3: _____, _____, and _____.

3. The _____ should be visible so that you _____ get disoriented.

4. The difference between drafting and modeling is the addition of the _____.

5. There are two ways to build on an existing part: _____ and _____.

6. The simplest method for creating a part from a profile is to _____ it.

Matching

7. Match the definitions with the correct options from the Extrude dialog box.

Definition	**Option**
_____ Specifies the overall length of the extrusion.	a. Operation
_____ Allows you to taper the extrusion.	b. Extents
_____ Used to reverse the direction of the extrusion.	c. Negative Z
	d. Distance
_____ Specifies the method of generating the extrusion. You have Join, Cut, and Intersect	e. More
	f. Graphic Generic Image
_____ Used to determine how the extrusion will be ended. Some of the options are To and From–To.	

True or False

8. The Angle option in the Revolve dialog box is used to set the complete angle of revolution desired.   T or F

9. The More tab of the Sweep dialog box allows you to specify whether you are a mesomorph, an ectomorph, or an endomorph.   T or F

10. Once you've identified the plane on which you'll be working, the 3D Indicator re-orients itself to align to the current working surface.   T or F

Multiple Choice

11. Sweep starts with both a:
    a. part and a path
    b. part and a profile
    c. path and a profile
    d. path and a fixed origin point
    e. none of the above

12. When creating your beginning sketches, you are working:
    a. in 3D
    b. in 2D
    c. beyond a planar surface
    d. with a Z axis
    e. b and d

What?

1. Explain the purpose and the operation of the right-hand rule.

2. Why is it important to have one fixed and one nonfixed orientation system?

3. What are the advantages of the Shade mode and of the Wireframe mode?

4. Explain the three buttons that control the direction of the extrusion.

5. Why do you use an isometric display when generating sketch features?

6. What function can a construction line serve in the creation of the part through revolve?

7. Explain the purpose of the 3D Indicator and the Coordinate System Indicator.

 # Let's Get Busy!

1. Create an extruded part using the Collar Clamp (CLAMPPRO) profile you created in Chapter 2, Assignment 3. Figures 3.26(a) and (b) illustrate what it should look like. Create a layer called Extrusion and give it the color cyan. The extrusion should start with a distance of 2. Remember to use an isometric view so that you can see the profile and extrusion.

    Once it has been extruded, use the Edit Feature tool and change the extruded distance to 3. Save this part as CLAMP.

Figure 3.26
Extruded Collar Clamp

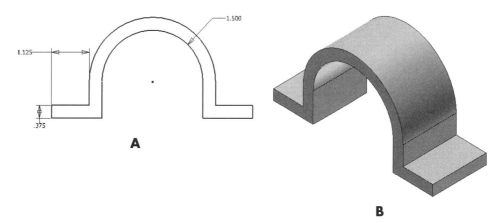

2. Create an extruded part using the Pivot Joint (PIVOTPPRO) profile you created in Chapter 2, Assignment 4. Figures 3.27(a) and (b) illustrate what it should look like. The extrusion should start with a distance of 3. Remember to use an isometric view so that you can see the profile and extrusion.

   Once it has been extruded, use the Edit Feature tool and change the extruded distance to 2. Save this part as PIVOT.

3. Create a 360° revolved part of a slip-on flange. You will need to create the profile first and dimension it. Then, using the REVOLVE command, turn it into a flange. Figures 3.28(a) and (b) show the profile and the final revolved shape. Save the part as FLANGESO.

4. Create a 180° revolved part of a motor casing as shown in Figure 3.29(d). First, you'll need to create the profile and dimension it as shown in Figure 3.29(a). If you use lines and fillets, you'll find that the profile will have all the necessary geometric constraints. Then, using the REVOLVE command, turn it into a half-round casing. Figure 3.29(b) shows the shaded isometric view.

   Next, you'll have to create a rectangular profile that will be used to cut out a half hole in the casing. Create the rectangle profile and dimension it as shown in Figure 3.29(c). First, with no command active, right-click in the graphics screen and pick New Sketch. Move the cursor near the bottom edge of the part until there is a red line highlighting the profile of the bottom of the part. Pick to use this to set the new sketch plane. Use the REVOLVE command with the Cut option to cut the revolved rectangle away from the original casing. Figure 3.29(d) shows the dialog box settings and the preview of the revolution. Figure 3.29(e) shows the outcome. Save the part as MCASING.

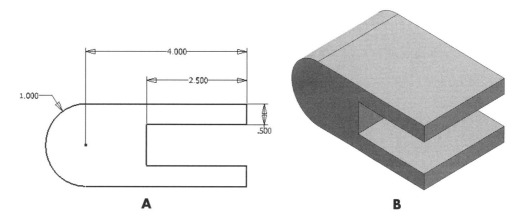

Figure 3.27   Extruded Pivot Joint

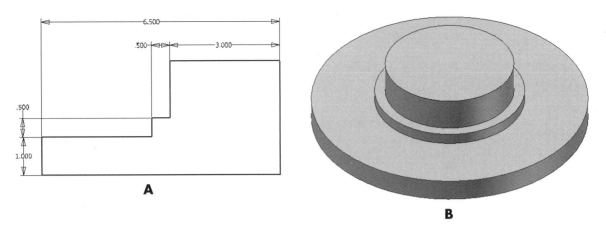

Figure 3.28 Slip-on flange profile and revolved shape

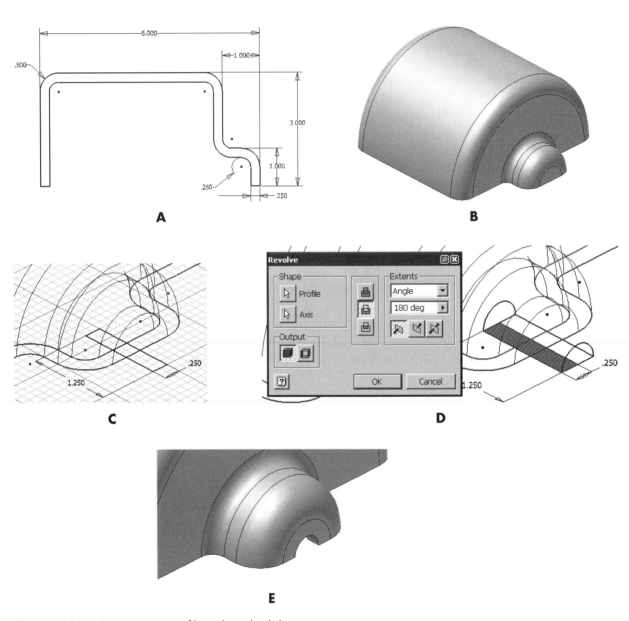

Figure 3.29 Motor casing profile and revolved shape

70

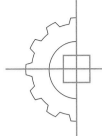

Chapter 4

Viewing and Working in 3D

Key Concepts

- Common Views
- Free Rotate
- Isometric View
- Shade Modes
- Sketch Planes
- Look At
- Work Features

Where Are You?

The key to the creation of complex parts is to know where your visual orientation is in relation to the part you want to create and on what working planes the creation is going to take place. This chapter introduces you to more advanced concepts relating to working in 3D. These involve viewing the 3D model in different ways and the creation of working surfaces that allow you to create on any axis.

Viewing in 3D

When you physically hold a part in your hand, you are able to turn it around and view it from any angle. You can see the relationships each side or surface has with another. It helps you to understand the part better so that you are able to refine or alter it with more confidence.

It is much the same experience when using Autodesk Inventor. However, instead of moving the part, you move your viewing location. You can think of it as though the part were suspended in mid-air and you're able to walk around it, looking at it from above or below. Figure 4.1 shows the same part from different viewpoints and shade modes. In this way you're able to see all around your part or model as you design it.

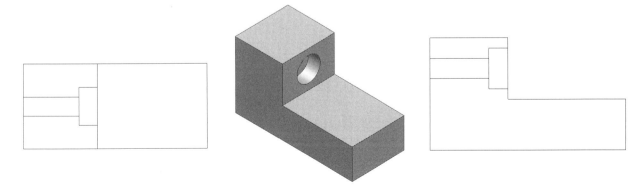

Figure 4.1   Various viewpoints and shade modes of a part

Think of it as though the part were suspended in mid-air and you're able to walk around it, looking at it from above or below.

The first step in viewing in 3D is understanding the relationship between the various sides of your part or model. If you've already had exposure to creating mechanical drawings, then you already know of the term *third-angle projection*. It refers to the viewing pattern of a part (see Figure 4.2). The three-dimensional part is being displayed orthographically showing the top, front, and right-side views. These are the customary views of a mechanical-type drawing. When you create a profile, you need to decide on which plane you're going to create your base profile shape and whether it is going to be a profile in the top, front, or side plane. Ultimately you can create on any plane at any angle. But as a beginner, it is easier to start with one of the three common planes.

Common Views

There are several methods of moving around your model to display it from different viewpoints. One of the easiest is to use the Rotate tool with the Common View option. This allows you to pick common viewpoints around your model, such as top, front, and right side.

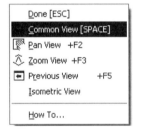

To access the command, pick the Rotate tool from the Standard toolbar. Right-click to bring up the context menu and select Common View from the menu. *Note:* If the Common View mode is already active, it will be replaced with the Free Rotate option in the menu. In Common View mode, a shaded gray cube will appear with green arrows pointing to various viewpoints on the cube. Figure 4.3(a) shows the Common View cube and arrows overlaid on a part. This is called the 3D View Direction Selector. When you pick one of the arrows, the view rotates to that viewpoint (see Figure 4.3(b)). Orthographic views are indicated by arrows pointing to the sides of the cube. Isometric views are indicated by arrows pointing toward the corners of the cube.

Figure 4.2 Typical orthographic views from 3D part

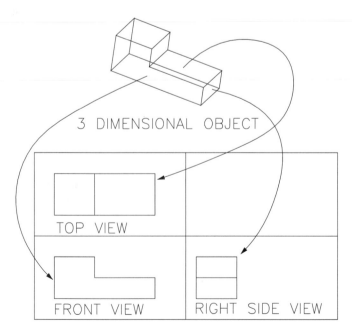

Figure 4.3 Using the Common View option/mode

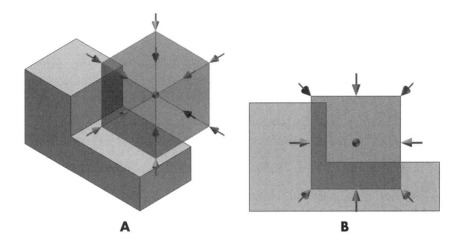

A   B

Free Rotate

A visually interactive method for displaying a view of the model can be found by using the Free Rotate mode/option of the Rotate tool. As with the Common Views option, pick the Rotate tool. If the Free Rotate mode is active, a large gray circle with various tab lines will appear over your model, which is referred to as the 3D Rotate symbol. If the 3D View Direction Selector cube appears instead, right-click and select Free Rotate from the context menu. The line tabs on the large circle are used to select the direction of view rotation (see Figure 4.4).

When you move your cursor around, inside, or on the four tab lines, the cursor changes to reflect the type of viewing rotation represented. Depending on where you pick and drag your cursor, the view will rotate to a new position (see Figure 4.4). The following describe the rotation axes.

Circular   When you move the cursor outside the 3D Rotate symbol, the cursor changes to a circular arrow. When you pick and drag around the outside of the 3D Rotate symbol the view rotation takes place around an axis that is perpendicular to the viewing plane or screen. When you release the pick button, the view rotation stops.

Figure 4.4 Active 3DORBIT command showing 3D Rotate symbol with sample cursors added

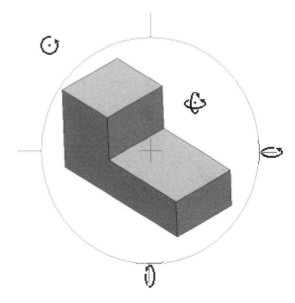

Center of Rotation

When using the Free Rotation mode, you can indicate where you want the center of rotation to be by picking inside the circle or outside near the circle. The view will pan centering on the location you picked.

 Horizontal   When you move the cursor into one of the tab lines on the left or right side of the 3D Rotate symbol, the cursor changes to a horizontal, elliptical arrow. When you pick and drag left or right, the view rotation takes place around a vertical axis that is parallel to the viewing plane or screen. When you release the pick button, the view rotation stops.

 Vertical   When you move the cursor into one of the tab lines on the top or bottom of the 3D Rotate symbol, the cursor changes to a vertical elliptical arrow. When you pick and drag up or down, the view rotation takes place around a horizontal axis that is parallel to the viewing plane or screen. When you release the pick button, the view rotation stops.

 Spherical   When you move the cursor inside the 3D Rotate symbol, the cursor changes to a combination of the horizontal elliptical arrow and vertical elliptical arrow. When you pick and drag inside the 3D Rotate symbol, the view rotation takes place around both axes. When you release the pick button, the view rotation stops.

Look At

 The Look At tool is a quick way to display an orthographic (flat) view of a particular surface or sketch on the part. Pick the Look At tool and pick the surface or sketch that you want to view perpendicular/flat to the screen. You may need to display an isometric view to be able to select the surface you want to view.

Zoom Selected

 The Zoom Selected tool allows you to enlarge the view of a selected element until it fills the screen. This can be particularly useful when you want to focus on one element on a complex part.

Displaying and Setting the Default Isometric View

A quick way to display an isometric view is to right-click and select Isometric View from the context menu. This default isometric view can be set to any of the six common isometric views by displaying the 3D View Direction Selector. Pick the arrow that displays the isometric view you want and then right-click and select Redefine Isometric from the context menu.

Display Modes Revisited

Display modes control how the part is displayed in a graphics screen. Normally it is easier to display a wireframe for construction and use various forms of shading for visually examining the shape of the part or model. If you pick and hold the Shaded Display tool, a flyout appears. The following is a description of each tool used to display a different mode.

	Shade	The surfaces of the model are shaded (colored) to give the model a solid look.
	Hidden Edges	The addition of highlighted, hidden edges are added to the shaded model.
	Wireframe	The part is shown so that all the edges appear as wires. The model is shown in a skeleton form.

Material Styles

Initially, when a part is created and shown shaded, it's given a default material style. This can be changed at any time to a material style that you want the part to be.

To assign a material style to a part, highlight the part by selecting its name in Browser and then select Materials from the Format pull-down menu. The Materials dialog box appears as shown in Figure 4.5.

The Material List lists the materials available. When you highlight a material from the list, its properties are displayed on the left. This does not assign the material to the part.

At the bottom of the dialog box is the Part Material drop-down list. Selecting a material from this list assigns the material to the object.

Note the Rendering Style drop-down list at the bottom of the Properties area. This sets how the part will be rendered/shaded on the screen. By default the rendering/color styles have been assigned to various materials. However, you can change these at any time or create your own material and assign a new rendering/color style.

Figure 4.5
Materials dialog box

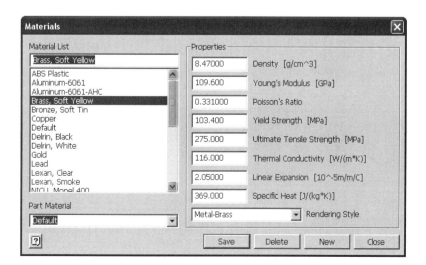

Color Styles

The color style can be useful to depict the part more realistically and make it easier to identify individual parts in a large assembly. Color styles are referred to as Rendering Styles in the Materials dialog box.

You can also change the color style of individual surfaces. This can be used effectively to differentiate between machined and nonmachined surfaces. Figure 4.6 shows a part that's cast with various machined surfaces. The cast surfaces are rougher and reflect less light. Machined surfaces are smoother and reflect more light.

To create a color style for a part, select Colors from the Format pull-down menu. The Colors dialog box appears as shown in Figure 4.7. To create your own color style, highlight one from the list and then pick the New button. You can then name the color style and then make adjustments to the settings.

You can also add a texture bitmap image to a color style to make the color style even more realistic. To do this, open the Texture tab as shown in Figure 4.8(a) and pick the Choose button. The Texture Chooser dialog box appears, allowing you to select a bitmap image to apply to the color style (see Figure 4.8(b)). The Cast Iron color style was created for this textbook. You will practice this in the next exercise.

Figure 4.6 Two color styles added to a part

Figure 4.7 Colors dialog box

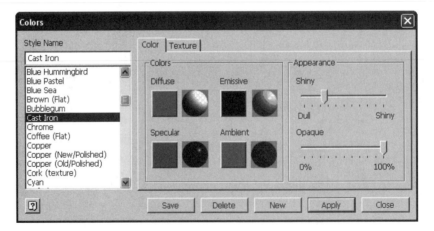

Figure 4.8
Assigning a Texture to a
color style

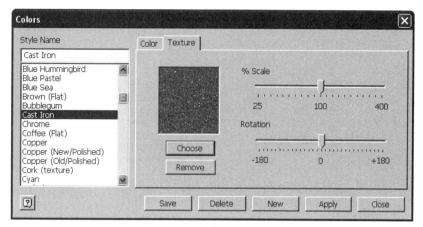

A

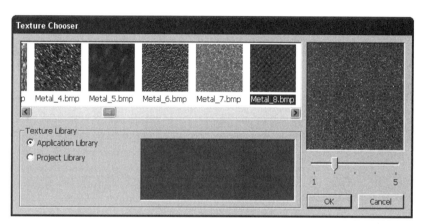

B

Surface Materials

To assign a color style to an individual surface, highlight the surface by picking it in the graphics screen. Select Colors from the Format pull-down menu and pick a color style from the list in the Colors dialog box. The color style will be added to the surface and will override the color style assigned to the entire part by its material.

Hands-On: Viewing in 3D

This exercise will provide practice in the use of the various methods of viewing a 3D model.

1.   Open the part file invex4A. This file contains a simple part to which you'll apply different view methods and materials. The screen should be similar to Figure 4.9(a).

Figure 4.9 Simple part and 3D View Direction Selector

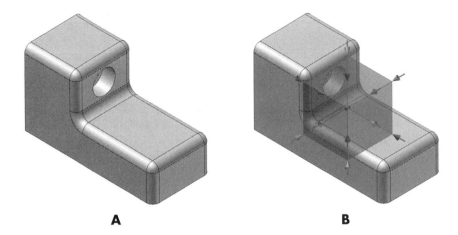

A   B

Using Common Views

2.   Pick the Rotate tool on the Standard toolbar. Depending on what rotation mode you're in, the free rotate circle may appear or the common view 3D View Direction Selector cube. For this part of the exercise, we want you to practice with the 3D View Direction Selector cube. If the cube is visible, advance to Step 3 now. If the cube is not visible, right-click and pick Common View from the context menu. The screen should now look similar to Figure 4.9(b).

3.   Observe where the green arrows point. Some point to corners (indicating isometric views) and some point to surfaces (indicating orthographic views).

Also note the orientation of the 3D Indicator located in the lower-left corner of the screen. The blue arrow points toward the positive Z axis, the green arrow points toward the positive Y axis and the red arrow points toward the positive X axis. You'll see in a few moments that the part does not move in relation to the axis. It's the viewpoint that moves.

Pick the arrow that points to the right surface of the 3D View Direction Selector cube. The right-side view should now be displayed similar to Figure 4.10.

Observe the 3D Indicator axes. The viewpoint has changed but the relationship between the axes and the part remains the same. Remember, the part is not moving. It's the viewer orientation that's moving.

Experiment with the other possible common views until you're comfortable moving around the part.

4.   Display a top view and exit from the ROTATE command. You may need to zoom out so that the part is smaller on the screen.

Using Free Rotate

5.   Pick the Rotate tool again. Right-click and pick Free Rotate from the context menu. The screen should now look similar to Figure 4.11.

6.   Move your cursor around the 3D Rotate large circle. Pause on the inside and outside and observe the shape of the cursor. Refer back to Figure 4.4. Identify the different cursor shapes. Move the cursor into each of the small tab lines and match the cursor shape to Figure 4.4.

Move the cursor into the bottom small tab line so that the cursor is displayed as the vertical elliptical arrow. Pick, hold, and drag the cursor upward and then downward but keep the pick button pressed. Note how the view of the part rotates. Display a view similar to Figure 4.12(a).

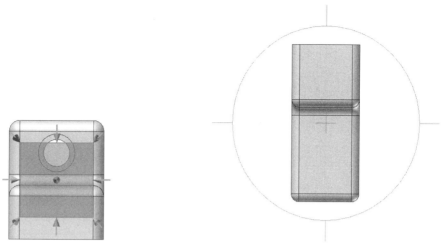

Figure 4.10   Right-side view   **Figure 4.11**   3D Rotate Symbol and top view

Figure 4.12
Rotating the view using
Free Rotate

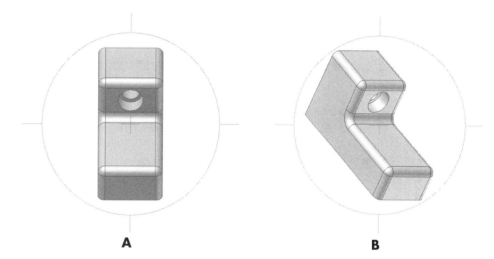

A   B

Now pick in the right small tab line, hold, and drag left and right. Observe the rotation of the part. Display a view similar to Figure 4.12(b).

Experiment with the other cursor shapes to revolve the view.

Color Styles and Materials

7.   Display an isometric view of the part.

8.   You're going to create a new color style called Casting-Steel.

Open the Format pull-down menu and select Colors. Note a dialog box similar to Figure 4.13. Scroll down and highlight the Mild-Steel color style and then pick the New button to make a copy of the highlighted style.

Observe that the style name at the top of the dialog box is now Copy of Mild-Steel. Change this to Casting-Steel.

Open the Texture tab and pick the Choose button. The Texture Chooser dialog box appears as shown in Figure 4.14. Scroll across and highlight the Metal_11.bmp texture bitmap image. This is the texture image that you're going

Figure 4.13 Colors
dialog box

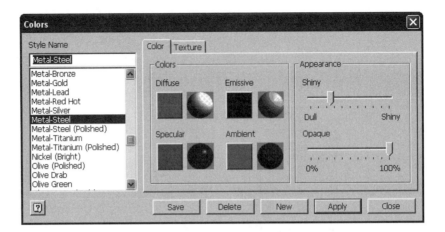

Figure 4.14 Texture
Chooser dialog box

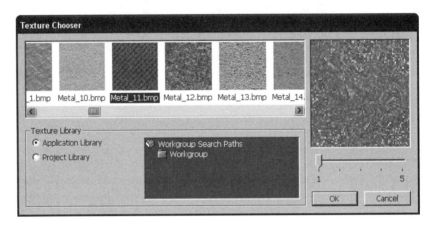

to apply to your part. It will simulate the rough texture of a casting. Once the image is highlighted, pick the OK button to continue.

The Texture tab should still be open. Adjust the % Scale slider until it's approximately 251%. This changes the scale of the bitmap image applied to the part.

Pick the Save button to save the color style and pick Close to close the dialog box. Don't pick the Apply button.

9. You're going to create a new material style called Steel-Casting and add your new color style to it.

Open the Format pull-down menu and select Materials. A dialog box similar to Figure 4.15 appears. Scroll down and highlight the Steel, Mild color style and then pick the New button to make a copy of the highlighted style. Change the new copy's name to Steel-Casting and then change the Rendering Style to your new color style Casting-Steel. Pick the Save button to add the new materials style and the Close button to close the dialog box.

10. The next step is to apply the new material style to the part.

Right-click on the name of the part in Browser. The part will turn blue in the graphics window and the context menu will appear. Select Properties from the context menu. The Properties dialog box for the selected part will appear similar to Figure 4.16.

Open the Physical tab and select Casting-Steel from the drop-down list. This time pick the Apply button and the OK button. Pick in open space in the graphics widow to dehighlight the part in blue. The part should now be shown in a different material, similar to Figure 4.17.

Figure 4.15
Materials dialog box

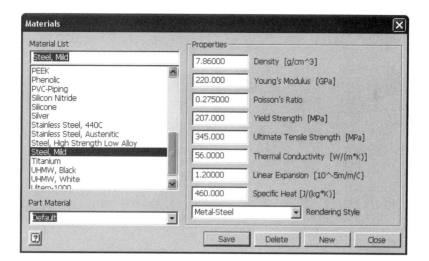

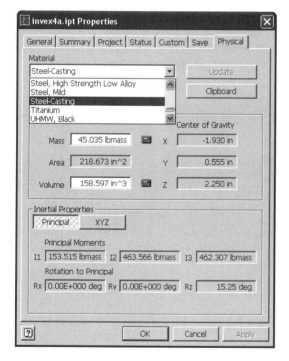

Figure 4.16   Properties dialog box

Figure 4.17   Casting material
applied to part

Surface Specific Color Styles

11. A casting is initially rough all over. However, wherever a surface is machined, it becomes smoother and shinier. The holes, the base, and the left side of the part are machined. These surfaces should appear smoother and shinier. You're going to apply color styles to those surfaces that are different from the rest of the part.

Move your cursor slowly over the hole in the part. A red outline of the counterbore hole will appear. Pick and the counterbore hole will turn blue, highlighting it. Right-click and select Properties from the context menu. The Face Properties dialog box appears, similar to Figure 4.18. Scroll down the list and

Figure 4.18 Face Properties

Figure 4.19 Applying a shiny color style to various surfaces

select Metal-Steel (polished). Pick the button to apply it to the selected surface. You should notice that the surface is now shiny, signifying a smooth finish.

Proceed to change the face properties of the entire hole, the base and the left side so that they are shiny as well. *Note:* If you hold down the Ctrl key when you pick surfaces, it will allow you to pick more that one at a time. You can see the appearance of the underside and left side of the part in Figure 4.19.

12. Save a copy of the part file as Ex4A.

Working in 3D

To create complex parts or models you have to be able to work on different planes and axes in 3D. As mentioned in Chapter 3 all construction in 3D is still based on a flat (planar) 2D plane. In this section you will learn how to create this plane, referred to as the sketch plane, as well as other forms of planes and axes.

Sketch Planes

To create any object in Autodesk Inventor, you must use a sketch plane. This plane stretches to infinity in all directions and is composed of the X and Y axes, which define the plane, and the Z axis perpendicular to the plane. There is only one sketch plane at any given time. You can create a new sketch plane from the drop-down menu located in the Standard toolbar or by right-clicking when no command is active. There are two types of sketches: the 2D sketch and the 3D sketch. Most of your construction will be using 2D sketches; 3D sketches are used for creation of more convoluted shapes such as pipe or cable runs that can move in several axes at one time.

2D Sketch Planes

Initially when you start a new part, a sketch plane is created for you. It's based on the Part settings in the Options dialog box (see Figure 4.20(a)). Normally, you would create the first sketch and then a base feature from the sketch. Once you have a base feature, you can create other sketch planes.

When you start a new sketch plane, you're prompted to select a *plane* to create the sketch plane. This *plane* can be a planar face on an existing feature or a work plane.

Figure 4.20   Part settings showing initial sketch plane

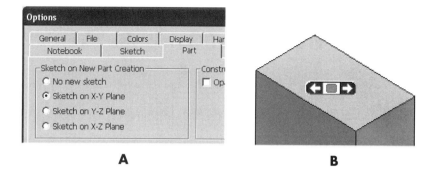

A   **B**

A sketch plane stretches to infinity in all directions.

Planar Face   You can align the sketch plane to any planar face on your part. As you move the cursor over the part, different faces will be highlighted by a red outline. If you pause on a face and there is a possibility that other faces could be selected, a cycle tool will be displayed as shown in Figure 4.20(b). Picking on the arrows cycles through the various surfaces. When the one you want is highlighted, move the cursor to the center; it will light up green and you can pick it. And, *ta dah*, the new sketch plane is defined. A blue outline identifies the face that you picked and a new sketch object is added to Browser. From there you can start creating the new sketch.

Work Plane   The creation of work planes will be discussed later in this section. It is enough to say at this point that there are other planes that you can add to the model to refer to during construction. You can align the sketch plane to previously created work planes.

3D Sketches

The 3D sketch environment is used to create 3D paths. These 3D paths are used to create 3D sweep features that define parts such as wiring, cabling, and tubing. When you activate the 3D sketch environment, the panel changes to show the 3D Sketch tools (see Figure 4.21). A 3D sketch does not require a plane to work from; however, it does need existing geometry to snap to. What this means is that as you create a line path, you snap to various locations on the existing part.

Figure 4.21   3D Sketch tool panel

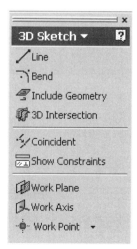

Hands-On: Moving the Sketch Plane

In this exercise you're going to move the sketch plane around the part and create sketches on different surfaces.

1. Open file invex4B. The file contains a simple object with several work planes.

2. Make sure your Sketch options (Tools/Application Options pull-down menu) are set as shown in Figure 4.22. Make sure that the isometric view is displayed.

Sketch Plane Moved onto Planar Face

3. The first method to change the sketch plane is to align it to a surface (planar face) on the part.

Select the 2D Sketch Plane tool and move the cursor over the part. When you're near an acceptable sketch plane object, the line that defines the plane becomes red.

Move your cursor until it is near the top of the part. When a red profile outlines the top face, pick it. A blue profile identifies where the new sketch plane is located and the coordinate system indicator shows the orientation.

Display a view parallel to the top surface by using the Look At tool. The resulting view should be similar to Figure 4.23(a).

Figure 4.22
Options dialog box showing sketch settings

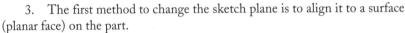

Figure 4.23 Circle profile dimensioned and extruded holes

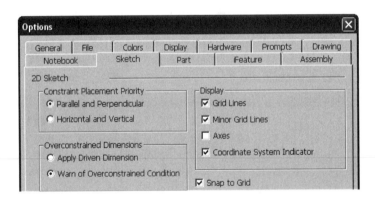
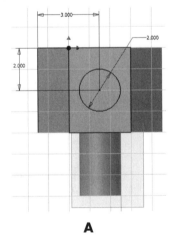

A   B

Figure 4.24
Extrude dialog box

4. Now draw a circle on the new sketch plane in the middle of the top surface with a radius of 1. Dimension the circle as shown in Figure 4.23(a) and complete the sketch by right-clicking, with no command active, and selecting Finish Sketch from the context menu.

5. Display an isometric view and select the Extrude tool. The Extrude dialog box will appear, similar to Figure 4.24. Use the Profile pick tool to highlight the circle. The area of the circle should turn blue if selected properly. Match your settings to Figure 4.24 and pick OK. The circle profile should now have cut a hole from top to bottom.

6. Now, move the sketch plane to the nearest sloped surface in the isometric view. Use the same technique you used for the top view.

7. On the new sketch plane, add a circle (0.5 radius) and extrude/cut it through the part. Your part should look similar to Figure 4.23(b).

Sketch Plane Moved onto Work Planes

You're now going to move the sketch plane to the work planes. Work planes are used when you want to create a sketch plane in a location where you would not normally be able to select a planar face. In this case, two work planes have been created tangent to the protruding cylinder. (Work planes are explained in detail in the next section of the chapter.)

8. Select the 2D Sketch tool and move your cursor over WorkPlane1 in Browser. When WorkPlane1 is highlighted, pick it.

9. The sketch plane is now aligned with the work plane. Both are parallel to the side view. Use the Look At tool to display the view of WorkPlane1. One way is to select the tool and pick WorkPlane1 in the browser.

10. Draw a circle (0.5 radius) on the new sketch plane so that it's approximately centered on the cylinder (see Figure 4.25 for its location). Finish the sketch.

11. Display an isometric view and use the Extrude tool to cut the circle through the cylinder. You may have to use the Flip button to ensure that the extrude arrow points inward, through the part.

Figure 4.25   Axes
for sketch plane on
work plane

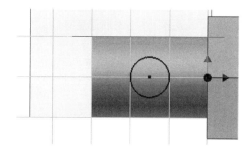

Figure 4.26
Shaded isometric view
with holes in cylinder

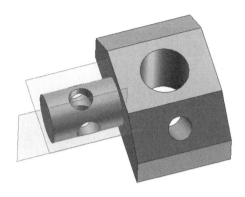

12. Perform the same procedure with the horizontal work plane (Work-plane2). Your part should look similar to Figure 4.26.

13. Save your ex4B part file.

You now know how sketch planes are used and how work planes can assist with the placement of a sketch plane. The next section explains the use of work features of which work planes are just a part.

Work Features

Work features are used to aid in the construction of the part or model. They can be used to define edges, planes, axes, or points. For instance, you can use them as an axis to create a revolved feature. There are three types of work features: work planes, work axes, and work points.

Work Planes

 A work plane is used to create an artificial face on which a feature can be built (see Figure 4.27).

Work features are used when a location is not readily accessible on the part you're contructing.

Figure 4.27   A part
showing a work plane

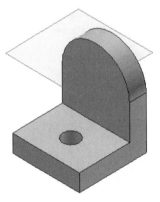

When you activate the command, the cursor changes to a pick arrow with a small plane symbol. This is prompting you to select geometry to define the work plane. This requires at least two geometric objects to form the plane relationship; these can be vertices, edges, faces, or other work features.

To define the relationship, you select a combination of objects. For example, you could pick a planar (flat) surface and then a vertex (point) on a corner of the planar surface. This would establish the work plane on the surface and indicate its location. If you selected two planar surfaces that were parallel but not in line, the work plane would be created an equal distance between them. You can use one or more of the following relationships to define a work plane:

- on geometry using three points
- normal (perpendicular) to geometry using an axis and a plane with an angle of 90°
- parallel to geometry using a plane and a point or two planes
- at an angle to geometry using a plane and an axis with an angle other that 90°

Work Axis

A work axis is a parametric line that is not normally part of the physical part (see Figure 4.28). With this axis, you can specify the centers of cylindrical or symmetrical objects and use the work axis as a reference point for dimensions. They can be used for such items as the axis on revolved features or polar arrays.

When you activate the Work Axis tool, the cursor changes to a pick arrow with a small axis symbol. This is prompting you to select geometry to define the work plane. You can select cylindrical objects, two vertices, or an edge.

Work Point

A work point is used to create a coordinate point on the model that is not normally part of the physical model. You can use the work point as a reference point.

To add a work point, you can select a vertex, a combination of an edge and a face, three faces that intersect, or a combination using work planes. Using work points is particularly useful when combined with drawing a 3D sketch. You can draw the sketch line through the various work points that you previously placed. Figure 4.29 illustrates a work point.

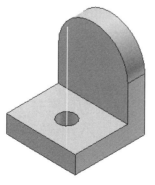

Figure 4.28   A part showing a work axis

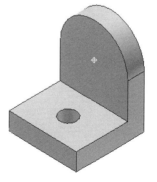

Figure 4.29   A part showing a work point

Hands-On: Creating Work Features

In this exercise, you're going to create two work features: a work plane and a work axis. Using these aids, you'll add more features to your part. Figure 4.30 shows the completed angle support.

1.   Open file invex4C. There are already some features added that you will work with. Also, note the profile. You will use this profile to create a sketched feature.

Work Plane

You're going to create a work plane that is tangent to the top arc in order that you can have a sketch plane to use to create a hole through the top.

2.   Select the Work Plane tool from the Part Features panel.

Move your cursor over the part and rest it on the top curved surface. The surface should be highlighted in red (see Figure 4.31(a)). Pick the surface. It will be used as the tangent face.

Move your cursor down to the top of the bottom base. A red rectangle will appear around it and a faint rectangular plane will appear tangent to the top (see Figure 4.31(b)). Pick the base face and the new work plane will be created as shown in Figure 4.31(c). The work plane should now have been created tangent to the top of the arc and parallel to the base.

3.   Create a new 2D sketch plane using the new work plane as the selection plane. You'll need to pick one of the edges of the work plane to select it.

Figure 4.30
Completed angle support

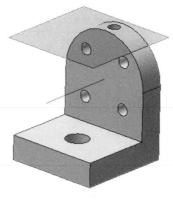

Figure 4.31
Creating a work plane on a curved surface

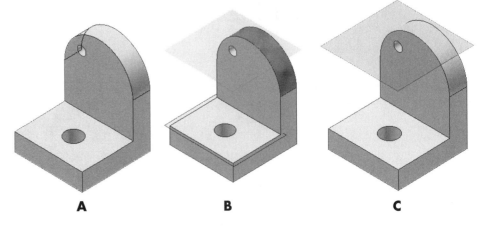

A   B   C

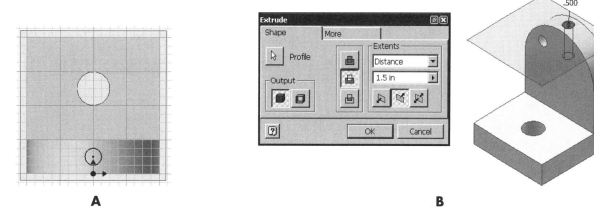

Figure 4.32   Sketching the circle, Extrusion dialog box, and the results

Using the Look At tool, display a top view of the part as shown in Figure 4.32(a).

Draw a circle with a radius of 0.25 in the center of the curved top (see Figure 4.32(a)). Finish the sketch to return to Part mode and display an isometric view.

4.   Use the EXTRUDE tool to cut the circle into the arc for a distance of 1.5 (see Figure 4.32). You'll have to use the Profile button to select the circle. When properly selected, the entire area of the circle will turn blue. You may have to flip the Z axis to cut into the part.

Work Axis

You're now going to create a work axis that runs through the center of the semi-circle. This axis will be used to create a circular pattern.

5.   Select the Work Axis tool from the Part Features panel.

Move your cursor over the part and rest it on the top of the curved surface. The surface should be highlighted red (see Figure 4.33(a)). Pick the surface. The work axis line will appear through its center. You may have to rotate the view slightly to see the axis line (see Figure 4.33(b)).

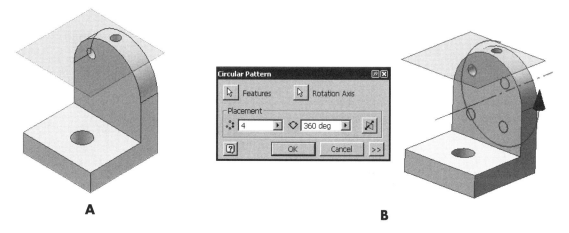

Figure 4.33   Adding the work axis, the Circular Pattern dialog box, and the results

6.   Select the Circular Pattern tool from the Part Features panel. The dialog box will appear as in Figure 4.33(b). Using the Features tool, pick the small hole in the upright face. Using the Rotation Axis tool, pick the work axis. Change the Placement number to 4. Figure 4.33(b) shows the dialog box settings and the preview pattern of the part. Pick the OK button to accept the settings and the new holes should appear.

7.   The result should look similar to Figure 4.30.

8.   Save a copy of the part file as Anglesup. Close the exercise file.

Desktop Visibility

To aid in the clarity of designing, Autodesk Inventor has a pull-down menu list used to control the display of various objects in your model such as work planes. You'll find it under Object Visibility in the View pull-down menu (see Figure 4.34(a)). You can then decide which object group you would like to be hidden from view or displayed. You can also hide or display individual work features by right-clicking on the feature name in the browser and then turning on or off the Visibility menu item from the context menu (see Figure 4.34(b)).

In a Nutshell

Being able to view your part from various viewpoints is an important part of the design process. Using various tools, you can display isometric or orthographic views. Displaying the part in wireframe will aid construction, while shading the part can help with visual interpretation. The creation of work features can help with the creation of objects and the placement of dimensions where there is no physical object to reference.

Now that you're able to create sketch planes anywhere on the model, you can move on to the addition of placed features such as holes and fillets and advanced creation through Cut, Join, and Intersect. These are covered in Chapter 5. After Chapter 5, you should be able to create complex parts.

Visibility of Work Features

Sometimes your part or model can get cluttered with various work features. You can control the visibility of an individual work feature by right-clicking on its name in the browser. From the presented context menu, you can turn visibility on or off.

Figure 4.34   Object visibility through pull-down menu and context menu

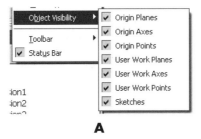

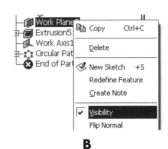

A   B

Testing . . . testing . . . 1, 2, 3

Short Answer

1. The Free Rotate command activates the _____, which is represented by a large circle.
2. Common View is a(n) _____ Free Rotate.
3. The four operations of the Free Rotate command are: _____, _____, _____, and _____.
4. The _____ tool is a quick way to display an orthographic (flat) view of a particular surface or sketch on the part.
5. Color styles are referred to as _____ styles in the Materials dialog box.

True or False

6. A sketch plane stretches to infinity along the X, Y, and Z axes.   T   or   F
7. Object visibility involves a procedure to make various objects, like work features, visible or invisible depending on the need.   T   or   F

Multiple Choice

8. The sketch plane must be aligned to the
   a. work plane.
   b. UCS.
   c. WCS.
   d. part's primary planar surface.
   e. all of the above
9. The work features include the
   a. work dot and the work plane.
   b. work point and the work line.
   c. work axis and the work face.
   d. work point and the work axis.
   e. work dot and the work axis.

What?

1. What is the function of the Look At tool?

2. What is the main advantage of using Free Rotate?

3. What is the main advantage of Common View mode?

4. List the four options of Free Rotate and describe how they work.

5. What function does the Zoom Selected tool perform?

6. List and explain the Display modes.

7. Explain the various choices for aligning the sketch plane.

8. What is a work plane? How does it differ from a sketch plane?

9. Why might you want to hide the display of work features?

Let's Get Busy!

1. Create the slide part shown in Figures 4.35(a) and (b). It has an extrusion distance of 3. Create a new sketch plane on the sloped surface and draw a circle on that plane. Save your file as Slide.

2. Create the wedge part shown in Figures 4.36(a) and (b). It has an extrusion distance of 4. Practice creating sketch planes on the various surfaces and draw a rectangle on each one. Save your file as Wedge.

3. Create the angle part shown in Figure 4.37. Scale is unimportant. Practice creating work planes on the various surfaces and then align the sketch plane to each one in turn. Refer to the figure for the work planes. Part (a) shows an isometric view and Part (b) shows a side view to help identify the sketch planes. Save your file as Angle.

4. Create the valve part shown in Figure 4.38(a). Create a construction line as shown in Figure 4.38(a). The distance the construction line is away from the edge of the profile will control the inside diameter of the hole and, as a result, the outside diameter of the valve. Use a distance of 1 as shown in the figure. Use the REVOLVE command to create a part with a construction line as the axis of revolution as shown in Figure 4.38(b). Save your file as Valve.

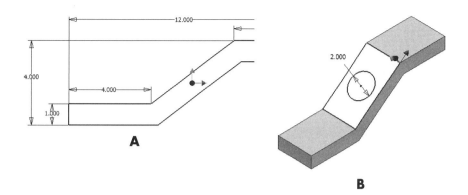

Figure 4.35 Profile and shaded slide part

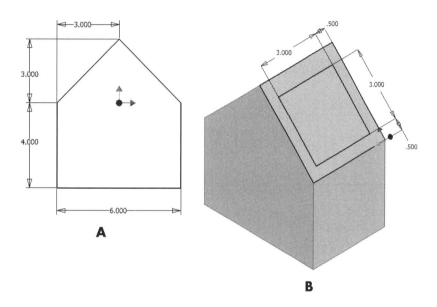

Figure 4.36 Profile and shade wedge part

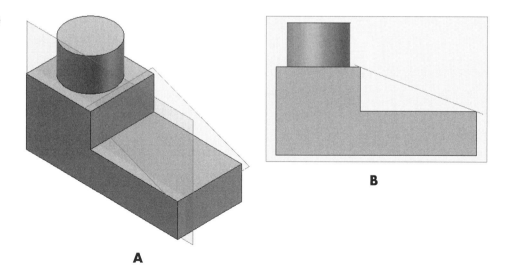

Figure 4.37 Angle

93

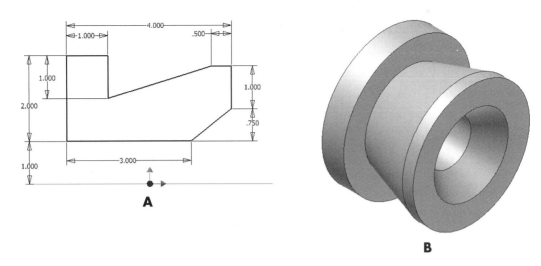

Figure 4.38 Profile and shaded valve part

Chapter 5

Part Editing

Key Concepts

- ◆ Editing Sketches
- ◆ Editing Features
- ◆ Building with Sketched Features
- ◆ Using Placed Features—Holes, Fillets, Chamfers, Shells, and Arrays

Making Waves

Now that you know how to create a base part and are able to create sketch planes, you're ready for more advanced creation—editing the base part. The first step is learning the methods to edit an existing sketch or feature; the next step uses sketched features to add or alter the base part; lastly, you will apply placed features such as holes or fillets.

At the completion of this chapter, you should be able to create almost any complex part that you want. From there, you'll move on to the creation of both drawings and assemblies.

Editing Sketches

The power of Autodesk Inventor lies in its ability to make changes or alterations after the fact. There are several methods that can be used to alter a part after it has been created, from editing a feature to editing the sketch used to create a feature.

You have probably noticed that when you take your sketch and create a part by using a sketch feature, such as extrude, the initial sketch disappears. The sketch is not really gone but rather has been imbedded into the sketch feature. Figure 5.1 shows a multi-featured part and Browser. Look down the expanded list and make note of the various sketches indicated there. You can edit any one of those to make changes to the initial sketch shape.

The power of Autodesk Inventor lies in its ability to make changes or alterations after the fact.

To edit a sketch contained inside a feature, highlight the name of the sketch located inside the browser. You may have to expand a feature level to see the sketch name. Once you have located the sketch name, right-click on the name and a context menu appears as shown in Figure 5.2(a). When you pick Edit Sketch, the sketch and the dimensions related to it appear as shown in Figure 5.2(b). You can double-click on any dimension value to make a change and the Edit Dimension dialog box will appear as shown in Figure 5.2(b).

Figure 5.1   Browser
and part

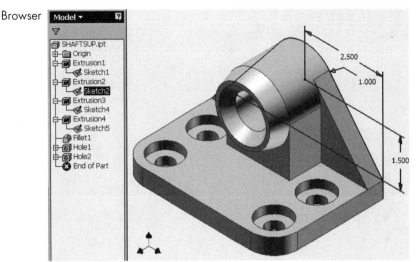

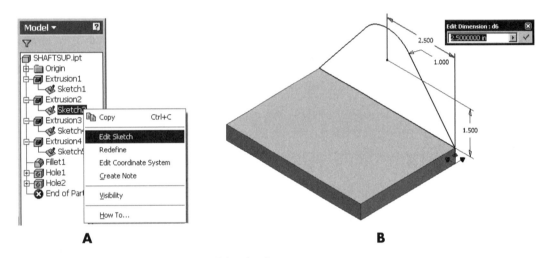

Figure 5.2   Sketch context menu and the sketch

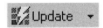

When you finish editing, the feature using the sketch will not change until you use the Update Part tool or close the sketch by selecting Finish sketch from the context menu. This incorporates your sketch changes into the part.

When editing the sketch, the sketch plane changes to match the sketch.

Editing Features

Features can be edited and changed anytime during the design process. Because all the information about a feature is stored, you can access and change that information.

To edit a feature, right-click on the feature name in the browser and select Edit Feature from the context menu. A dialog box similar to the one used to create the feature will appear. Figure 5.3 shows the dialog box overlaid on the part. You can then make the change and OK it. Usually the part will update automatically when a feature is changed. If you notice that the Update button is active, pick on it to update the part.

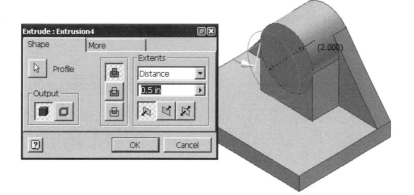

Figure 5.3 Dialog box used to edit feature and the part

Fast Editing

To quickly edit a sketch or feature, double-click on the sketch or feature name in the browser. The sketch or the feature dimensions appears immediately.

Features can be edited and changed anytime during the design process.

If you select Edit Sketch, the part disappears and the sketch appears for you to edit. There is also a Suppress option located in the Feature Context menu. The Suppress option will remove the feature from the part; however, it is not deleted. You can bring the feature back by unsuppressing it. Suppressing a feature is used sometimes to aid in the construction of a part by causing the part to revert to a stage before the feature was added.

Hands-On: Editing Sketches and Features

1. Open file invex5A. A part similar to Figure 5.4(a) will appear.

2. Expand the hierarchy in the browser so that you can see all the items, as in Figure 5.4(b).

Sketch Edit

3. Right-click on Sketch1 in the browser and select Edit Sketch. The part should disappear and the sketch and its dimensions should appear.

4. Return to the part by using the Update tool.

5. Right-click on Sketch1 in the browser and this time select Visibility. The part should not disappear and the sketch and its dimensions should appear over top.

Double-click the overall length dimension of 9. Change it to 5 and press Enter twice to exit from the command. Note that the sketch changed but the part did not.

6. Incorporate the change into the part by using the Update tool.

Figure 5.4 Initial part and expanded hierarchy

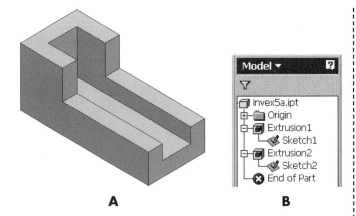

A   B

Feature Edit

7.   Right-click on Extrusion2 in the browser and select Edit Feature from the context menu. The Extrude dialog box will appear. Change the distance value from 8 to 3 and OK it. The command will finish. Note how the part was updated automatically. This will sometimes happen when you are editing features.

8.   Save a copy of the part file as EX5A.

9.   Experiment with altering other dimensions on both sketches and features.

Building on the Design with Sketched Features

Usually you employ a sketch feature to create a base part from a profile. This defines the basic shape of the part. Once you have the base part, you can use additional sketch features to refine the design. You can join, cut, and intersect features with the base part and with each other to create a complex part. There is no limit to the number of sketched features you can add. Figure 5.5 shows the base feature and the profile, and the three common Boolean operations using a sketch feature: Join, Cut, and Intersect.

The procedure to create a new sketch feature on an existing part is as follows (see Figure 5.6).

1.   Establish a sketch plane on the desired surface of the part.
2.   Create a sketch on the sketch plane. Add geometric constraints to the profile and add dimensions as required. Right-click to use the context menu to select Finish at the end of the creation of the sketch.
3.   Apply the desired sketched feature. (When entering the options for a new sketched feature, you're now able to join, cut, or intersect with the base feature.)

Figure 5.5 The base feature and the three Boolean operations using a sketch feature

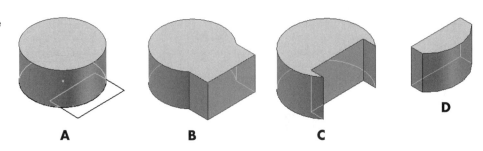

A   B   C   D

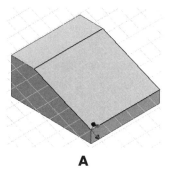

A

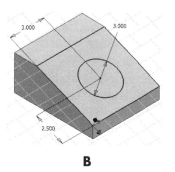

3.000   3.000

2.500

B

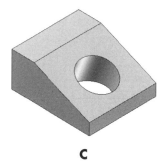

C

Figure 5.6   Procedure to add a new sketched feature

Order of Operations

You can create a part in any order to arrive at the final design. However, the process can be simplified greatly if you review the part to be designed and break it down into various stages or shapes. A good idea is to sketch out (on paper) the part creation as a series of frames or figures representing the stages, outlining the creation of the part.

Hands-On: Joining Sketched Features

In this exercise, you're going to create a shaft support as shown in Figure 5.7. This will involve using EXTRUDE with the Join option.

1.   Open file invex5B. This file contains the initial profile.
2.   Using the EXTRUDE command, extrude the profile a distance of 0.5. This will be the base feature.

There is no limit to the number of sketched features you can add.

Figure 5.7   Shaded view of completed shaft support

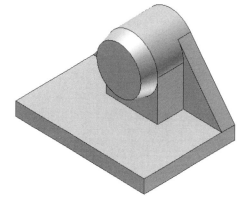

☑ Sketch ▾

3.   Create a sketch plane on the back face of the base feature as shown in Figure 5.8. You will have to use the Free Rotate tool to turn the base feature around so that you can see the back.

4.   Display the rear view and draw a circle as shown in Figure 5.9(a) with the dimensions and location as shown in Figure 5.9(c).

Add two lines tangent to the circle as shown in Figure 5.9(b). To do this draw a line that starts from the lower corner of the extruded base. Drag the end of the line onto the circle and move slowly around the circle until the tangent symbol appears, then pick. Repeat for the other side.

Trim the circle using the Trim tool and dimension as shown in Figure 5.9(c). Right-click when complete and select Finish Sketch from the context menu.

5.   Using the EXTRUDE command, extrude the new profile a distance of 0.5. Use the Join option to join the new feature to the base feature (see Figure 5.9(d)).

6.   Move the sketch plane to the front of the new extruded feature.

Figure 5.8   Sketch plane on back face

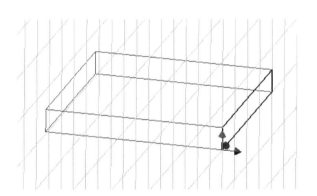

Figure 5.9   Profile sketch: (a) initial circle, (b) tangent lines and base line, (c) trim and dimensions, (d) extrusion

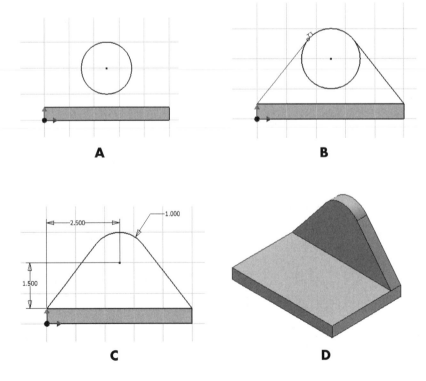

Figure 5.10 Profile and extrusion

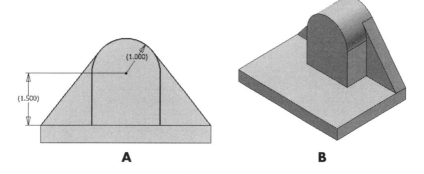

A   B

Figure 5.11 Profile and extrusion

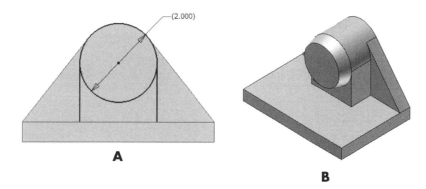

A   B

7. Create a new sketch as shown in Figure 5.10(a) and dimension it. Right-click when complete and select Finish Sketch from the context menu.

8. Using the EXTRUDE command, extrude the new sketch a distance of 1. Use the Join option to join the new feature to the second extrusion (see Figure 5.10(b)).

9. Move the sketch plane to the front of the new extruded feature.

10. Create a circle with a radius of 2. Its center should match the center of the arc on the second extruded feature as shown in Figure 5.11(a). Turn it into a profile and dimension it on the Dim layer.

11. Using the EXTRUDE command, extrude the circle a distance of 0.5 on the Extrude layer. Use the Join option to join the new feature to the second extrusion. Also add a draft angle of −15 degrees (see Figure 5.11(b)).

12. Shade the isometric view. Your part should be similar to Figure 5.7.

13. Save a copy of the part file as Shaftsup.

Placed Features

Placed features are features that are created automatically without the need of a profile sketch. These include such items as holes, fillets, and chamfers. By entering design information in a dialog box, the feature is created to those specifications. This is extremely useful when applying counterbores or countersinks because of the simplicity of their application. Figure 5.12 shows a part with placed features added.

Figure 5.12   Part
with placed features
applied

Holes

Holes can create straight drilled holes, countersinks, or counterbore (see Figure 5.13(a)).
There is also a threads feature that allows you to specify the type of thread. When complete, a simulated thread is added to the hole on the screen when in Shade mode. If the
part is displayed in wireframe, the thread image is not shown. Figure 5.13(b) shows the
dialog box used to control the hole feature. The following describes the various areas:

Centers   The Centers tool is used to select a Point, Hole Center sketch object to
identify the location for the hole. If there is a hole center sketch object, it
will be automatically selected.

Operation   Selects the type of feature to create: Drill, Counterbored, or Countersink.
These are shown by three tools.

Termination   Selects the hole's ending point:

Distance—goes to a depth that you set, creating what is called a blind hole

Through All—goes through the entire part

To—sets the depth to a plane that you select

Figure 5.13
Different hole types and
the dialog box

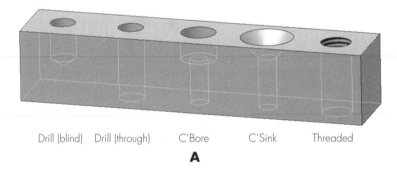

Drill (blind)   Drill (through)   C'Bore   C'Sink   Threaded

A

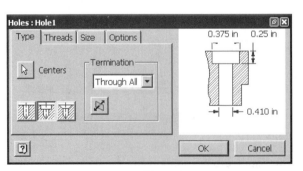

B

Hole Penetration

If you do not want a hole to penetrate all the way through an object, use the Distance termination option. If you want a hole to stop when it meets another hole or hollow, use the To termination option.

Size	This is set by picking on the various values shown in the graphic window contained within the dialog box.
Direction	The direction tool is used to switch the direction of the hole.
Threads	This tab/area is used to turn on the thread feature. You can make adjustments such as thread depth or right- or left-handed.
Size	This tab/area sets the size of the threads. It's automatically picked based on the diameter of the hole set under the Type tab.
Options	This tab/area is used to adjust the drill point and the countersink angle.

Hands-On: Adding Holes

In this exercise, you're going to add several types of holes to an existing part called a lock support. These will involve different termination points.

1.   Open file invex5C. Figure 5.14 shows the completed part with the added holes.

Countersink—Concentric/Through

2.   The first hole-placed feature will be a countersink that is placed in the center of the vertical cylinder. It will run completely through the part. Use the Sketch tool to set the sketch plane on the top face of the vertical cylinder. Use the Point, Hole Center toll to place a hole center sketch object in the center of the top face. Finish the sketch to return to the part mode.

Select the Hole tool and the Holes dialog box will appear. Use the Centers tool to select the newly created hole center sketch object. Match your settings to Figure 5.15 and pick the OK button.

Figure 5.14
Completed part with added holes

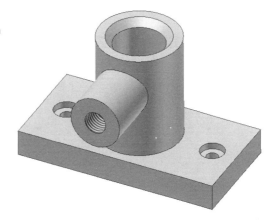

Figure 5.15 Hole dialog box and hole center sketch object on top of the cylinder

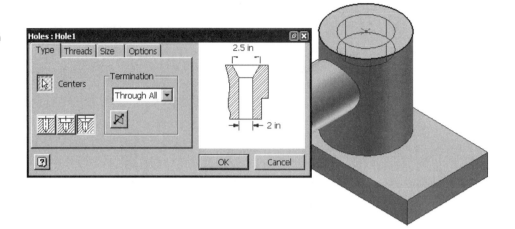

Drill—Concentric/Threaded

3.   The second hole-placed feature will be a drill/threaded that is placed in the center of the protruding horizontal cylinder. It will go from the flat face of the cylinder to the hole created by the countersink.

Use the Sketch tool to create a sketch plane on the front of the horizontal cylinder. Use the Point, Hole Center tool to place a hole center sketch object in the center of the front face. Finish the sketch to return to the Part mode.

Select the Hole tool and the Holes dialog box will appear. Use the Centers tool to select the newly created hole center sketch object and set the hole diameter to 1.0.

Set the termination to To. You'll need to pick the vertical hole as the termination point using the To tool. It will turn blue.

Open the Threads tab and turn on threads by checking the Tapped box. Also, turn on the Full Threads box. Return to the Type tab. Your settings should look similar to Figure 5.16.

Counterbore—2 Edges/Through

4.   The third and fourth holes will be counterbores that will be placed from the edges of the base plate. They will go through the plate. See Figure 5.17 for the settings. The hole will be placed 1 × 2. The next hole will be placed in the same way but from the opposite side.

Figure 5.16 Hole dialog box and hole center sketch object on front face of cylinder

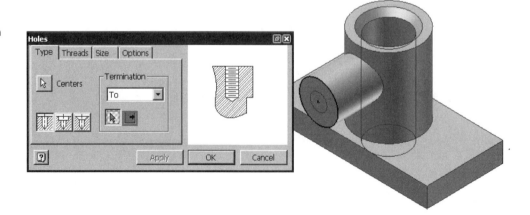

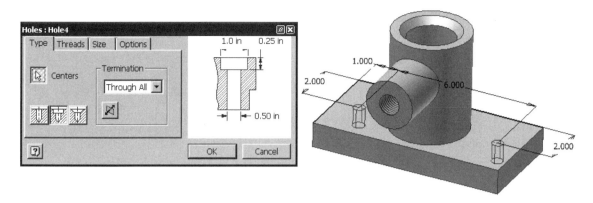

Figure 5.17   Hole dialog box and hole center sketch objects on top face of plate

Use the Sketch tool to create a sketch plane on top of the base plate. Use the Point, Hole Center tool to place two hole center sketch objects as shown in Figure 5.17(a). Dimension and Finish the sketch to return to the Part mode.

Select the Hole tool and the Holes dialog box will appear. The two hole centers should have been automatically picked. If they were not, use the Centers tool to select them. Match your settings to Figure 5.17. Note the threads setting may still be on; make sure you turn it off. Pick the OK button to add the holes.

5.   Save a copy of the part file as Locksup.

Fillets

To add a fillet, select the Fillet tool. You will be prompted with a dialog box similar to Figure 5.18. Initially you're expected to select the edges to blend (fillet). You can pick as many as you want and they will all be included under one group. Likewise, if you delete one fillet in the group, all the fillets are deleted.

If you think you might want to change the radius of fillets individually within a group, pick the gray *click to add* text in the edges box. If you think you might want to delete individual radii, create them as separate groups. You can edit a radius at any time by right-clicking on the fillet in the browser and selecting Edit Feature from the context menu.

Figure 5.18   Fillet
dialog box

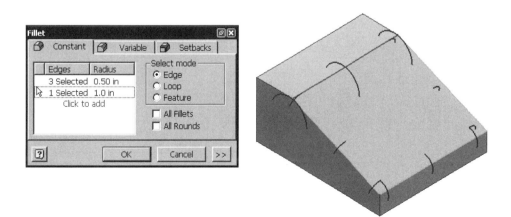

When to Add Fillets

Usually the rounding or filleting of edges on a design does not have any major effect on the overall design. Because of this, filleting can be left for last. This way, the part is greatly simplified until the very end, when numerous fillets can be added.

There are three types of fillets: constant, variable, and setback. Figure 5.19 shows the three types of fillets used on the same part.

Constant   A constant fillet has the same radius along its entire length (see Figure 5.19(a)).

Variable   A variable fillet has a different starting and ending radius. It can have a smooth radius transition as shown in Figure 5.19(b)). When smooth radius transition is turned off, the fillet is linear as shown in Figure 5.19(c)).

Setback   Setbacks are used to set a fillet back from a corner (see Figure 5.19(d)). Locate the fillet edge that is bolder. It has been set back more than the other two fillets.

Chamfers

The creation of chamfers is similar to the creation of fillets. Figure 5.20 shows the dialog box with the three methods of specifying the chamfer: equal distance, distance × angle, and two distances.

Figure 5.19   A part showing a combination of (a) constant, (b) variable smooth, (c) variable linear, and (d) setback

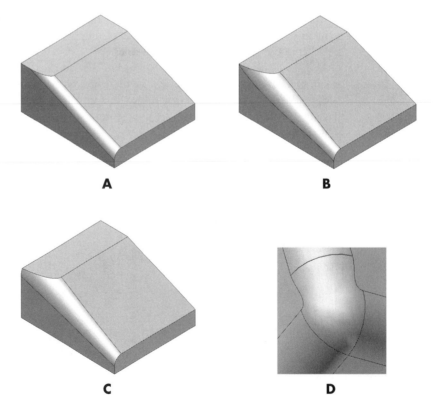

A

B

C

D

Figure 5.20
Chamfer dialog box
and part

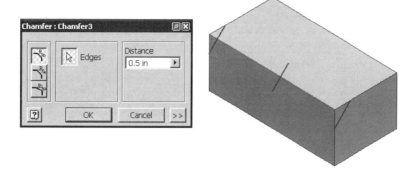

Hands-On: Applying 3D Fillets and Chamfers

In this exercise, you're going to practice adding 3D fillets and chamfers to a part.

1.   Open file invex5D. It represents a moulded part called a Vslide. It is missing some chamfers and fillets necessary to complete the part. Figure 5.21 shows the before and after images of the part.

Chamfers

2.   To add a chamfer, select the Chamfer tool; the dialog box will appear (see Figure 5.22). Set the chamfer to two distances and use the Edge tool to pick the edge. Set the distances to 1.0 and 0.5. You may have to use the Direction to switch the distances so that the 1 value is along the top surface. Pick OK to complete the chamfer. Apply the chamfer to the opposite edge.

Figure 5.21   The
before and after Vslide

Before

A

After

B

Figure 5.22
Chamfer dialog box
and the part

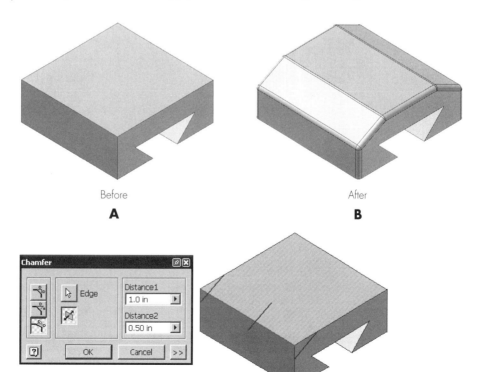

Figure 5.23 Fillet dialog box and the part

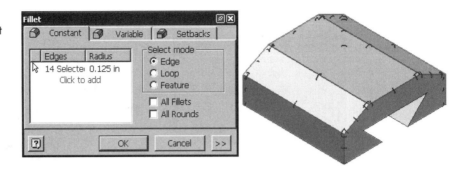

Fillets

You're now going to apply rounds to most of the edges using Autodesk Inventor's Fillet tool. The only edges that will remain sharp are the V groove and the bottom of the base. These represent surfaces that are machined. The rounded edges represent the moulded edges of the part.

3.   Select the 3D Fillet tool; the Fillet dialog box will appear. Set the values to match Figure 5.23. You're going to apply a constant fillet to all the edges around the part, except for the bottom of the base and the V groove. Pick OK to apply the fillets. Press Enter when done. The results should look similar to Figure 5.21(b).

4.   Save a copy of your file as VSLIDE.

5.   Experiment with the Edit Feature tool and modify the fillets and chamfers. Add other chamfers to see the results.

Shell

The shell-placed feature is a special type of feature. It modifies the part by adding a wall to the inside or outside of the part as shown in Figure 5.24. You can specify the thickness and the command will do the rest of the calculations needed to create the wall. Because the shell is added to the entire part, it can be applied only once on an individual part, though you can modify the wall thickness when desired; for example, you can use a constant wall thickness or multiple wall thicknesses.

The most important point to keep in mind is that the wall must be thin enough to be able to be created throughout the entire part. If the wall thickness is too large, interior features will be lost. If the part is too complex, the shell may not be created.

The following is an explanation of the Shell dialog box shown in Figure 5.25.

Figure 5.24 A part and the addition of a shell

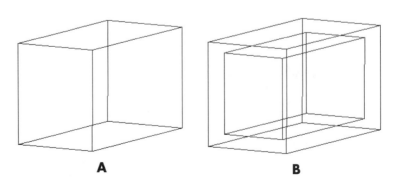

A   B

Figure 5.25   Shell dialog box

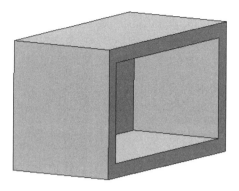

Figure 5.26   Creation of an open shell with front face excluded

Shell and Fillets

If you plan to create a shell on the inside of a part, keep this in mind when you're applying the external fillets. The external fillets should have a radius large enough to allow the adaption of the interior fillets of the shell. For example, if you fillet the outside of the part with 0.25 radius fillets and then apply a shell with 0.125 wall thickness, the interior shell fillets will be 0.125. If you used an exterior radius of 0.125 and a wall thickness of 0.125, there would be no room for the interior fillets.

Remove Faces   This tool is used to remove faces from a wall. This has the effect of creating an open shell (see Figure 5.26). The front face was excluded when the shell was created.

Thickness   Sets the thickness of the shell.

Direction tools   Three tools used to indicate whether the shell should be on the inside, outside, or both sides of the part.

Unique face thickness   Used to create different thicknesses on various walls of the shell.

The shell wall must be thin enough to be able to be created throughout the entire part.

Patterns

The patterns-placed feature creates multiple copies of an existing feature. Patterns were previously called arrays. You can create a rectangular pattern or a polar (circular) pattern. There are pattern tools for sketches as well as features. They function in a similar fashion. Figure 5.27 shows the dialog box, the part with patterned hole centers, and the result with hole features applied.

When using the Rectangular Pattern dialog box, you must select the geometry to be copied. As well, you need to select existing geometry that will be used to indicate the direction the pattern copies will take. Remember the number of copies includes the original.

Figure 5.27   Pattern
dialog box and the
results

Figure 5.27   Pattern
dialog box and the
results

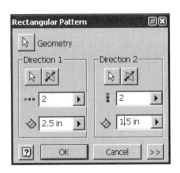

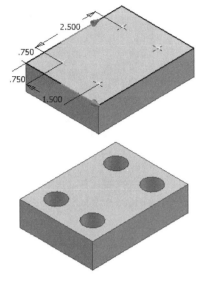

Figure 5.28   Pattern
dialog box and the
results

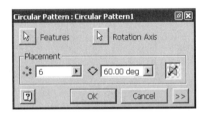

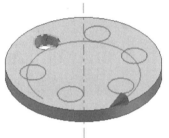

Figure 5.28 shows the Circular Pattern dialog box and the results. You must have a work axis or cylindrical feature already created before you can create a polar pattern. These features are used to specify the rotational axis of the circular pattern.

Like any other feature, you can edit the pattern feature. If you modify the original feature, all the copies will be modified as well.

Hands-On: Creating a Shell and Using Patterns

In this exercise, you're going to practice adding a shell to a solid part to turn it into a casing. You're also going to practice creating patterns.

Creating a Shell

1.   Open file invex5E. It shows an unfinished multimeter casing. You're going to add the shell to complete the upper half of the casing. Figure 5.29 shows the part with the shell added.

2.   Use Free Rotate to move around the part to see the underside. You should be able to tell that it's a completely solid part.

3.   Display a wireframe isometric view so that you can see the inside part.

A   **B**

Figure 5.29   Completed multimeter casing with the shell added

Figure 5.30   Shell dialog box

4. Select the Shell tool and the dialog box appears. Match your settings with that of Figure 5.30. This will create a shell throughout the inside of the part. OK the settings and observe the results.

Display a shaded view and move around the part, looking from below. There doesn't seem to be any change. This is because the shell was created entirely inside the part. What we want is to leave the bottom and the cutouts on the top open, without a shell.

5. Make sure that the display is set to shaded and an isometric view.

6. Highlight the Shell label in the browser. Right-click it and select Edit feature from the context menu. The Shell dialog box will appear again.

7. Note that in Figure 5.31 the Remove Faces button is depressed and the arrow is red. If it isn't, make it so.

Next, use your cursor to pick the two cutouts' bottom faces and the bottom face of the entire body. They will turn blue when picked correctly. You'll have to use Free Rotate to rotate the part so that you can pick these features. The Shell command will stay active when you use the Free Rotate command. Once you've picked the three faces, pick the OK button and observe the results.

8. Move around the part. You should be able to see through the cutouts and see the open face under the part. Your finished part should look similar to Figure 5.29.

9. Save a copy of your file as MCASE.

Creating Patterns

1. Open file invex5F. It shows the unfinished sprocket part. You're going to add the missing mounting holes and finish the creation of the teeth. Figure 5.32 shows the completed part.

Figure 5.31   Excluded faces from the shell

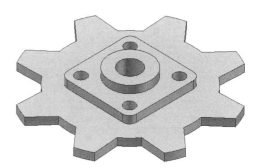

Figure 5.32   Completed sprocket part

Rectangular Pattern

You're first going to create a rectangular array of the small mounting hole that lies near the center of the part.

2.   Select the Rectangular Pattern tool and a dialog box will appear. Note that the Pick Features button is depressed. Pick the small hole feature on the graphics screen. It should be profiled in blue.

Depress the Pick Direction 1 button and select one of the edges of the part. This sets the direction that pattern will take in one direction. Repeat with the Pick Direction 2 button. Figure 5.33 shows the direction arrows.

You may have to use the Switch Direction tools to change the arrow direction to suit the figure.

Match your settings with that of Figure 5.33(a). Remember that the original feature is considered one of the copies in the pattern. OK the dialog box and the results should look like Figure 5.33(b).

Circular Pattern

You're now going to create a Circular pattern of the cutout on the perimeter of the sprocket circle. This will create the teeth.

3.   Select the Circular Pattern tool and the dialog box will appear. Note that the Pick Features button is depressed. Pick the cutout feature on the graphics screen. You may have to rotate the part to select it (see Figure 5.34). It should be profiled in blue.

Depress the Rotation Axis button and select center hole. The circular copies will rotate about this center. A blue centerline will appear (see Figure 5.34).

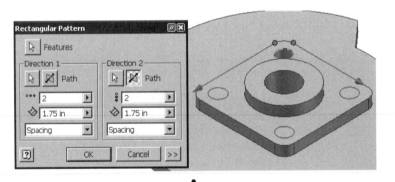

A

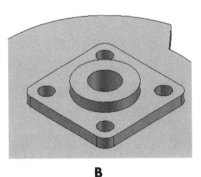

B

Figure 5.33   Rectangular Pattern dialog box and the results

Figure 5.34
Circular Pattern dialog
box (polar) and the
results

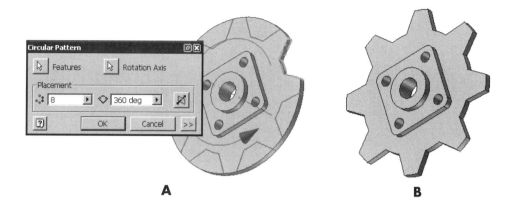

A   **B**

> Match your settings to Figure 5.34(a) and pick OK to continue. The cutout fea-
> ture will be copied around the perimeter and the results should look like Figure
> 5.34(b).
>
>   4.   Save a copy of your file as Sprocket. Display a shaded view; it should
> look similar to Figure 5.32.

Other Placed Features

Some other placed features are Face Draft, Split, Thicken, and Emboss.

Face Draft   Creates sloped faces on a selected feature. You first specify a pull direction.
              This identifies the direction of the slope. You then select the faces you
              want tapered to the draft angle.
Split   Splits and removes faces from a part. A work plane can be used to define
              the cut line.
Thicken   Creates an extruded feature from a selected face.
Emboss   Creates an embossed or engraved feature by using a sketch and projecting
              it onto a surface.

In a Nutshell

Autodesk Inventor's powerful editing commands make it possible to edit parts from the
features down to the base sketch. Once the base part is created, you can use join, cut, and
intersect sketched features to create more complex parts. The final addition to a part is
the application of placed features such as holes and fillets. These automatic features help
to speed up the design process many times over.

You now have the information needed to create complex parts of your own design.
The next step is to turn the part into a part drawing. This is covered in the next chapter.

Testing . . . testing . . . 1, 2, 3

Fill-in-the-Blanks

1. The _____ option is used at times to aid in the construction of a part by causing the part to revert to a stage before the feature is added.
2. You may have to expand a feature level to see the _____.
3. There are two methods to edit an object, by _____ on the object name in Browser or right-clicking on the object name in Browser to bring up the _____ .
4. The three common Boolean operations using a sketch feature are: _____, _____, and _____.
5. The Holes feature can create _____, _____, and _____.
6. There are four other placed features:

    _____ creates sloped faces on a selected feature. You first specify a pull direction. This identifies the direction of the slope. You then select the faces you want tapered to the draft angle.

    _____ splits and removes faces from a part. A work plane can be used to define the cut line.

    _____ creates an extruded feature from a selected face.

    _____ creates an embossed or engraved feature by using a sketch and projecting it onto a surface.

True or False

7. You can create a hole feature without a hole center sketch object.   T or F
8. A variable fillet can have a different starting and ending radius.   T or F
9. The Shell feature modifies the part by adding a wall to the inside or outside of the part.   T or F

Multiple Choice

10. Filleting should be
    a. done at the start.
    b. left for last.
    c. done at any time; it makes no difference.
    d. left to an expert.
11. The three methods of specifying a chamfer are:
    a. equal distance, two distances, and distance y angle.
    b. equal distance, distance y angle, and distance x angle.
    c. equal distance, two distances, and distance x angle.
    d. two distances, distance x angle, and distance y angle.
12. The features that are used to specify the center of a polar pattern include:
    a. a work axis or cylindrical feature.
    b. a work axis or working plane.
    c. a cylindrical, hole, or shell feature.
    d. a counterbore, a countersink, or a drilled straight hole.
    e. none of the above

Matching

13. Match the definition to the correct word by filling in the space with the appropriate lowercase letter.

_____ Constant
_____ Setback
_____ Variable (smooth transition)
_____ Variable (nonsmooth transition)

a. linear radius with a different start and end radius
b. a nonlinear radius with a different start and end radius
c. a radius that is moved back from the edge
d. has the same radius along its entire length

What?

1. Describe the procedure you must follow to edit a dimension on a base part from the first step to seeing the alteration on the screen.

2. What purpose does the Suppress option serve?

3. Why is it important to create counterbores and countersinks to exact specification by entering those specifications in the dialog box?

4. What is meant by a placed feature?

5. Describe some of the problems that come when creating a shell.

6. What is the procedure to create a circular pattern?

7. What are some possible uses for fillets and chamfers?

Let's Get Busy!

1. Add four holes to the collar clamp (CLAMP) that you extruded in Chapter 3, Assignment 1. Figure 5.35 shows the added holes.
2. Add fillets and holes to the pivot joint (PIVOT) that you extruded in Chapter 3, Assignment 1. Figure 5.36 shows the added fillets and holes.
3. Add fillets to the Lock Support (LOCKSUP) that you created in this chapter. Figure 5.37 shows the added fillets.
4. Create the strap clamp shown in Figure 5.38. This involves the use of Cut to create the slots, and Chamfers to create the sloped surfaces. Save the file as STRAP.
5. Create the die base shown in Figure 5.39. This involves the use of Cut to create the openings. Use Hole placed feature to create the two holes. Save the file as DIEBASE.
6. Create the miniature pneumatic cylinder body shown in Figure 5.40. This involves the use of Join and Cut when extruding, as well as the application of Hole features. You may want to apply fillets when you're finished. Save the file as MINICYL.

Figure 5.35   Collar clamp with added holes

Figure 5.36   Pivot joint with added fillets and holes

Figure 5.37   Lock support with added fillets and holes

Figure 5.38 Strap clamp

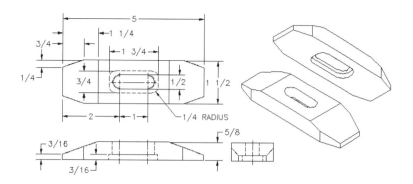

Figure 5.39 Die base

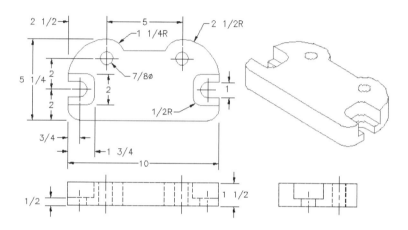

Figure 5.40
Miniature pneumatic cylinder body

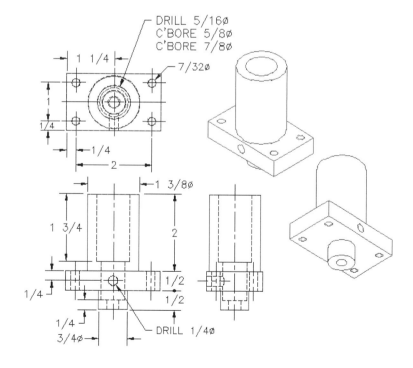

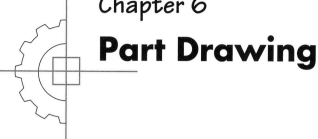

Chapter 6

Part Drawing

Key Concepts

- Creating Drawing Views
- Types of Views
- Adding, Moving, Hiding, and Editing Dimensions
- Hidden Lines and Centerlines

Little Things Mean a Lot—The Details

Once you've designed and created your part, you need to be able to present it to others. The typical way to do this is to generate a detail drawing of the part. From this drawing, the physical part can be manufactured. Figure 6.1 shows a detailed drawing of a modeled part. Drawing creation consists of four basic stages: formatting the drawing, creating drawing views, adding annotations, and printing/plotting a drawing.

This chapter deals with the methods used to go from a modeled part to a detailed drawing of that part.

Formatting the Drawing

Creation of a drawing occurs in the drawing environment. The first step is to start a new drawing. This can be done when first starting Autodesk Inventor or by picking New from the File pull-down menu.

Figure 6.1 Detailed drawing of modeled part

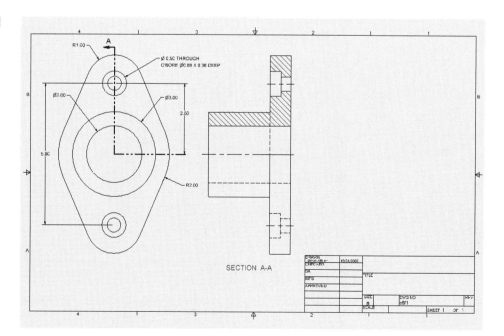

ANSI (in).idw

When the Open dialog box appears, pick the New tool on the right and open the appropriate tab. For this chapter, it's English.

From there, pick the ANSI (in).idw template. It contains the default drawing settings.

The program then opens the drawing environment and places a drawing sheet, border, and title block on the screen (see Figure 6.2). It shows the browser and the drawing layout in the drawing environment.

Drawing Format

When you select the drawing template to start a new drawing, the drawing standards are automatically set. This is great for the beginner. You can start creating drawings without worrying about all the various settings. However, if you want to customize a drawing, you can alter these standards using the Format pull-down menu. The following is a description of the menu items.

The Drafting Standards dialog box contains a list of drawing standards with one already selected based on the initial template. If you expand the dialog box, you'll see a series of tabs that contain all the settings of the drawing standard (see Figure 6.3).

The Dimension Styles dialog box allows you to modify existing styles or create a new one (see Figure 6.4).

The Text Styles dialog box allows you to modify exiting styles or create a new one (see Figure 6.5).

The Drawing Organizer dialog box is used to copy dimension and text styles from one drawing to another.

Once you've started a new drawing, you can change the sheet, border, or title block. If you right-click on the sheet name as in Sheet:1, you can select Edit Sheet from the context menu. This brings up the Edit Sheet dialog box. You can alter the sheet name, size, and orientation.

Under the Sheet:1 name is the border and title block used on the sheet. You can right-click on either and delete. Once deleted, you can add new ones.

Figure 6.2   The drawing environment

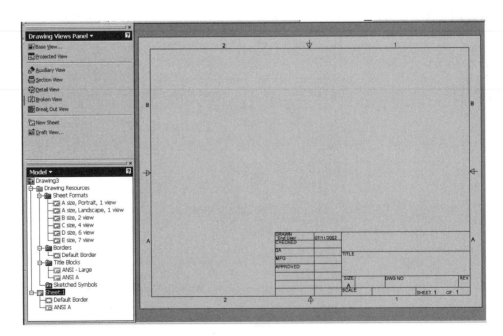

Figure 6.3 Drafting standards dialog box

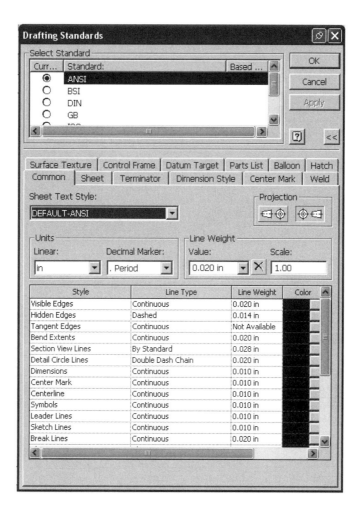

Figure 6.4
Dimension Styles dialog box

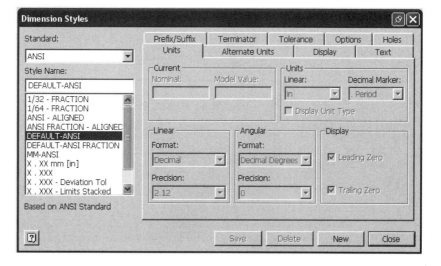

If you right-click on Default Border under Borders, you can select Insert Drawing Border. This brings up the Default Border Parameters dialog box.

You can insert either the ANSI A or ANSI Large title blocks by right-clicking on either name and selecting Insert.

Figure 6.5   Text
Styles dialog box

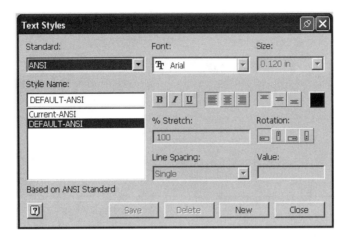

Multiple Drawings

You can have as many drawing sheets as you like in one file. Each one can reference a different part. Just use the New Sheet tool and a new empty drawing sheet will be added to the file.

Creating Drawing Views

Under your guidance, Autodesk Inventor will create the drawing views automatically from your 3D part. You start from a base view and then add the different types of views that you desire such as orthographic, auxiliary, or isometric. You simply indicate where the views will go and Autodesk Inventor does the rest, generating the appropriate view and adding the dimensions for you. The dimensions come from the specifications you used to create the part. You may find that all you have to do is alter the placement of the dimensions to complete the drawing. Even the hidden lines can be added automatically. Wow!

From the detail drawing, the physical part can be manufactured.

Another great feature is that the drawings will update automatically as you change your part. The information contained in the part and drawing are linked. If you change the part, the drawing will change to reflect your alterations. Conversely, if you change the drawing, the part will change. This allows for easier and quicker modifications.

The first step of this process is to transfer your 3D model into two-dimensional views. There are a variety of types of views that can be used to represent your part, allowing you a huge amount of flexibility in the layout of your drawing.

You can create single views one at a time or multiple views all at once.

View Type

There are seven basic view types: base, projected, auxiliary, section, detail, broken, and break out. You can add hidden lines to these views.

Base   The base view is the first view to be created since it is used to create other views. It is based on their location and viewpoint; you can pick from a top, front, or side view for the base view.

Projected   This is the typical orthographic view that is projected from another view, either horizontally, vertically, or isometrically.

Auxiliary   This is an auxiliary view that is created perpendicular to a selected edge on another view. It is typically used to view a slanted surface without distortion, as might happen with an orthographic view.

Section   This type of view represents either a full, half, offset, or aligned section view from another parent view. You can create a view cutting line while the Section tool is active, or create sketch geometry to use for the view cutting line.

Detail   The detail view is used to focus on a particular area of an existing view. For example, it is used to enlarge an area to be viewed more clearly, making it easier to refine a part's dimensions.

Broken   A broken view is used when you want to break away a portion of the center of a view but retain each end and the correct overall dimensions. This is used when a part may be very long and the interior portion of the part is not important to the manufacturing.

Break Out   A break out view removes a defined area of material to expose obscured parts or features in an existing drawing view. A sketch boundary is used to define the area to be exposed.

Options

The Options dialog box contains some settings that control the creation of drawings. Figure 6.6(a) shows the dialog box. There are also drawing settings contained in the Document Settings dialog box shown in Figure 6.6(b). Both dialog boxes are accessible from the Tools pull-down menu.

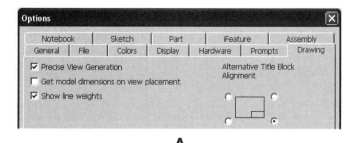

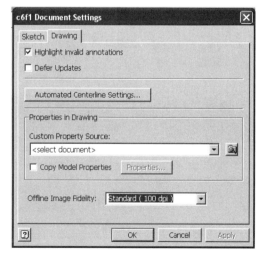

A   **B**

Figure 6.6   Options and Document Settings dialog boxes

ANSI (in).idw

Hands-On: Creating Drawing Views

In this exercise, you'll create various types of views and sections by making use of a part already created for you to practice on. Afterward, you can start creating your own drawings.

1.   Open file invex6A. It contains the Casting Base part already created for you.

The drawing environment is separate from the part environment; however, preloading the part saves the procedure of looking for the part in the drawing environment. When you start a new drawing, it knows that a part is also loaded.

2.   Save a copy of the file as CBASE. Close the invex6A file and open the new CBASE part file.

3.   Use the New command to start a new drawing file. Use the ANSI (in).idw template under the English tag. When it loads, immediately save it as CBASE.

A sheet, border, and title block will already be inserted automatically from the template file. Let's make some adjustments so that you're familiar with the process.

Drawing Format

4.   The sheet size is set to a C (17in × 22in) by default. It's too large for this part. You're going to change the sheet to a B (11 × 17).

Right-click on the Sheet:1 title in the browser and select Edit Sheet from the context menu. An Edit Sheet dialog box similar to Figure 6.7(a) should appear. Change the name of the sheet to Casting Detail and the size to B (see Figure 6.7(b)). Pick OK to complete.

Note in the browser that the sheet now reads Casting Detail.

5.   Use the Zoom Window tool and enlarge a view of the title block area.

Note that the Drawn box is filled in as well as Date, Sheet size, and Drawing Number. The drawing number is the file name. This is done automatically when you use the template file. Let's make some changes.

6.   Open the drawing properties by right-clicking on the drawing name CBASE in the browser and selecting Properties from the context menu. The Properties dialog box will appear. Open the Summary tab and change the author

Figure 6.7   Edit Sheet dialog box before and after changes

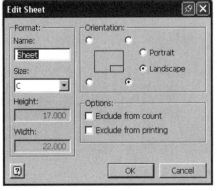

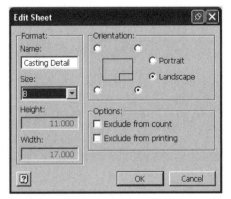

A   B

Figure 6.8
Properties dialog box

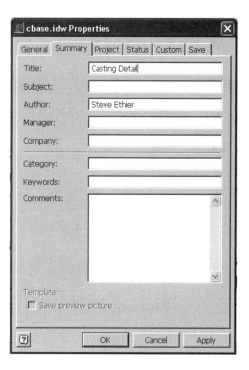

to your name and add the drawing title (see Figure 6.8). Open the Project tab and enter 0 as the revision number. Then pick the Apply button and the Close button to complete. The title block should have some of its information now filled in.

Use the Zoom All tool to fill the screen with the drawing sheet.

Standard Orthographic Views

7.   The first view you'll create is the base view. The other views will be based on it. It can be any type of view, such as top, front, or side. In this case, you're going to use the front view as the base view.

To create a single drawing view, pick the Base View tool and match your settings with the dialog box shown in Figure 6.9.

Note that the Orientation is set to Right. This sets the proper orientation for the base view. If you drag your cursor around the screen, you'll see that a view

Figure 6.9   Drawing View dialog box for base view

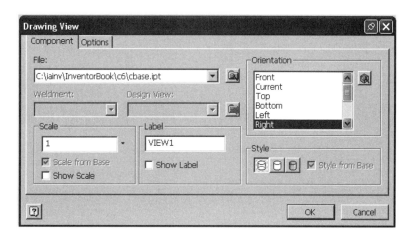

Figure 6.10   Placing
the view in paper space

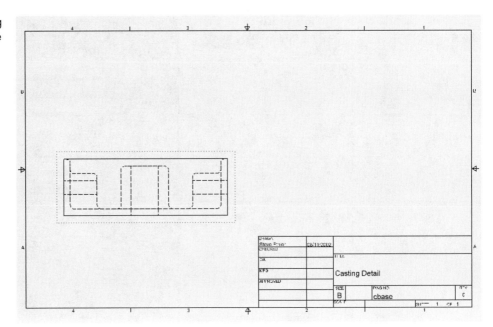

of the part is displayed. You can then place it where you want or pick OK and
move it afterwards. Pick the OK button to accept the view.

Move your cursor onto the view; a red dotted box will surround the view
and the four movement arrow cursor will appear. Pick and drag the view to a
location similar to Figure 6.10. As you can see, hidden lines were added automatically.

8.   To create the top view, pick the Projected View tool. A project view
from the base view will automatically appear.

Move your cursor around the base view and watch what happens. The project view will switch depending on the orientation of the cursor to the base view.
Move your cursor to generate a project top view. Refer to Figure 6.11 for the
placement and then pick to place that view. An empty box will appear at that
location.

Now you can move the cursor around and place other views (see Figure
6.12). When you've placed all the view boxes, right-click and select Create from
the context menu. The project views will now be created as shown in Figure
6.12. Go into the browser and rename them Top, Front, Right Side, and Isometric. Figure 6.13 shows the views renamed in the browser.

9.   Save your file as CBASE but don't close the drawing. Save a copy of your
drawing as CBASE2.

Figure 6.11   Placing
the projected top view

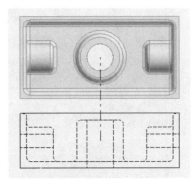

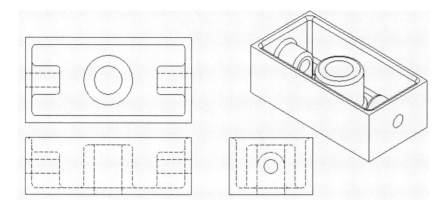

Figure 6.12   All projected views placed

Figure 6.13   Renamed views in the browser

Moving Views

If you're not happy with the location of the view after you have placed it, move your cursor onto the view and pick and drag. This will allow you to slide the orthographic view perpendicular to the parent view you selected. If you move the parent view, the other views will follow.

Section Views

10. Close the CBASE drawing and open CBASE2.

11. You're going to delete the front, side, and isometric views. Right-click the base view, Front, in the browser and select Delete from the context menu. A dialog box similar to Figure 6.14 will appear. Make sure the Top view is set to No for deletion. You want to keep this view. Pick OK and the Front and Right Side views should disappear leaving the Top view. Right-click the Isometric label and Delete that view as well.

12. Select the Section View tool and then pick the top view in the graphics screen on which to perform the section. You're then asked to draw the section line on the top view. Figure 6.15 shows where the section should be drawn.

The line should extend out from the geometry on each end of the view. Move your cursor to the center of one end of the view and pick. Then drag the

Figure 6.14   Delete View dialog box

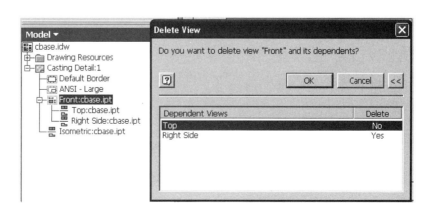

Figure 6.15 Section
View dialog box

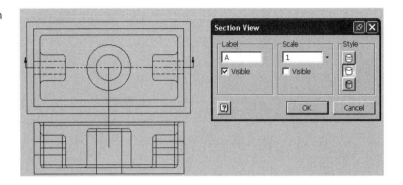

Figure 6.16
Completed section
views

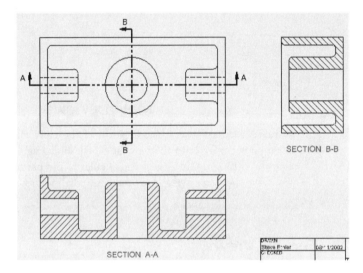

SECTION B-B

SECTION A-A

cursor to the other end and pick. This sets the cutting plane line of the section. Right-click and pick Continue.

The Section dialog box appears allowing you to set information about the section. Match your settings to Figure 6.15. Once you've done this, you can drag the section view into position and pick. Note how the section line appears in the top view and is labeled as well in the section view.

13. Repeat this procedure to generate a side section view. Unfortunately, you can't use the section front view. If you did, you would get half of a half section. Use the top view again and refer to Figure 6.16 to see the section line and final section views.

14. Save your drawing as CBASE2.

Section Views

You cannot create a section view from a parent section view. To get around this, create a new parent base view that is not sectioned. Use it to create the second section view. Delete the parent base view and re-create the first section view.

Drawing Dimensioning and Annotation

Autodesk Inventor can automatically add dimensions to a drawing view. The dimensions come from the ones you added when creating the part in the modeling stage.

There are two methods used to add the dimensions from your part model, by an Options setting or right-clicking on the view. If you refer back to Figure 6.6(a), you'll notice a setting: Get model dimensions on view placement. If this is turned on, dimensions will appear automatically when you place a view. The second method is highlighting a drawing view and right-clicking. From the context menu, open the Get Model Annotations flyout and pick Get Model Dimensions.

This causes the automatic addition of dimensions from the part model and can save you time; however, they're not always placed in the correct location. In fact, some of them you may not want to see at all. You may also find that you need to add more dimensions to clarify the part's manufacturing. The following section deals with these items.

Moving and Hiding Dimensions

To move a dimension, move your cursor over the dimension. It will turn red, and green circles will appear. Pick and drag the dimension text or the green circles to the new location.

To hide a dimension, right-click on the drawing view and open the Annotation Visibility cascading menu. From there, you can control the visibility of all the dimensions in that view.

If you want to hide an extension line, right-click on the extension line and select Hide Extension Line from the context menu.

The automatic addition of dimensions...can save you time; however, they're not always placed in the correct location.

Editing Drawing Dimensions

There are several ways to edit a dimension in a drawing. If you double-click the dimension, a Dimension Tolerance dialog box appears, as shown in Figure 6.17. Using this dialog box, you can add tolerances to the dimension value.

If you right-click the dimension and select Text from the context menu, the Format Text dialog box appears, as shown in Figure 6.18. Using this dialog box you can adjust the look of the text or add your own text. Note the <<>>; this represents the actual model dimension. You can add text before and after.

You can't delete the model dimension value. However, you can hide the model value by right-clicking the dimension and selecting Hide Value from the context menu.

Deleting Dimensions in a View

You can delete individual dimensions from a view without fear of changing the part model. Just pick the dimension to highlight it and press the Del key. The dimension lines and text are deleted from the drawing only.

Figure 6.17
Dimension Tolerance
dialog box

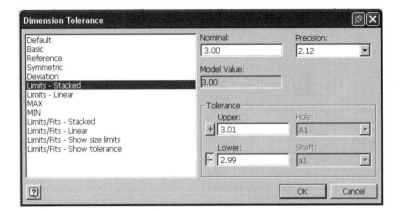

Figure 6.18   Format
Text dialog box

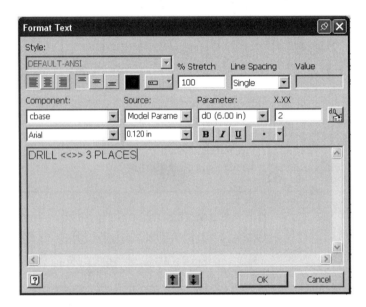

If you right-click the dimension and select Edit Model Dimension from the context menu, the Edit Dimension dialog box appears. You can then change the value and it will be applied to the model as well as the drawing. It sometimes takes a few minutes to update everything.

Drawing Annotation Panel

The Drawing Annotation Panel is used to add annotations to the views that are not added automatically. In this way you can add dimensions and hole notes exactly the way you want them to read. Figure 6.19 shows the panel. These annotations will be updated automatically should you modify the model.

Changing Dimensions on a Completed Part

Care must be taken when altering dimensions on a completed part. A changed dimension can affect other features on the part, especially fillets. Sometimes when you change a dimension on a part that is filleted, the fillets will be erased. You'll have to go back to the part model, delete the fillet operation, and add it back in again.

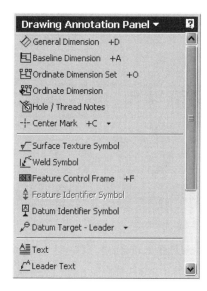

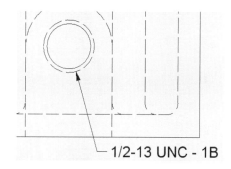

1/2-13 UNC - 1B

Figure 6.19   Drawing Annotation Panel   **Figure 6.20**   Threaded Hole Note

Hole/Thread Notes

Autodesk Inventor does not automatically display hole specification notes on the drawing, but you can add this information. To add a hole note, use the Hole/Thread Note tool.

When you use the tool, you'll be asked to select the hole feature, then, depending on the type of hole selected, the hole specification note will appear allowing you to position it. Figure 6.20 shows a threaded hole note. The information is taken from the part model file. Once the note is added, you can right-click and select Text to add more information to the note.

Annotations

To complete your drawing, you can annotate your drawing in various ways with the use of notes, leaders, geometric tolerances, and welding symbols.

To complete your drawing, you can annotate it in various ways with the use of notes, leaders, geometric tolerances, and welding symbols.

Hidden Lines and Centerlines

When you create a view, the lines that represent the edges, visible or hidden, are created automatically. You can control this creation during the creation of the view or afterwards by editing the view. Sometimes you want hidden lines to display and sometimes not, but usually hidden lines are not displayed on section views. *Note:* There are cases when hidden lines must be shown on a section view to clarify the placement of a particular feature.

To alter the display of hidden lines, right-click on the hidden line and select Visibility. The hidden line will become invisible.

Figure 6.21
Centerline Settings
dialog box

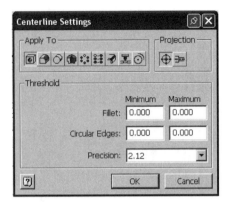

Hiding Edges from Display

Sometimes visible edges can hinder other lines, such as centerlines, on a section view. You can hide any edge on a view by right-clicking the line in the drawing and selecting Visibility. To redisplay the line, right-click on the view name in the browser and select Show Hidden Edges. You can then select which edges you want to redisplay.

Redisplaying the invisible hidden line requires the use of the browser. To restore a hidden line, right-click the view name in the browser and the context menu appears. If there are invisible hidden lines, the menu item Show Hidden Edges will be present. Select it. You will be prompted to move your cursor over the view and invisible hidden lines will appear red. Pick the ones you want visible again.

Centerlines can be added to the drawing in two ways: semi-automatically and manually. When you've added a view and you want to add centerlines, right-click the view and select Automated Centerlines. A dialog box similar to Figure 6.21 will appear. Using this dialog box, you can control which features and in which projection there will be centerlines. You can further adjust thresholds to eliminate certain sizes of features. Once you've adjusted your settings, pick the OK button and various centerlines will appear. This isn't always perfect. Certain features, even though circular, will not have automatic centerlines created. However, you can add them manually.

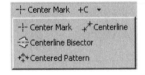

To add a centerline manually, use the Center Mark flyout in the Drawing Annotation Panel. From there, you can add center marks, add centerlines, bisect two edges, or create a circular centerline pattern.

Hands-On: Drawing Dimensions

In this exercise you'll alter the drawing you created in the last Hands-On. You'll add model dimensions and move their locations. You'll also add centerlines, other dimensions, and hole notes.

1.   Open file CBASE. This is the drawing you created showing three orthographic views and an isometric view.

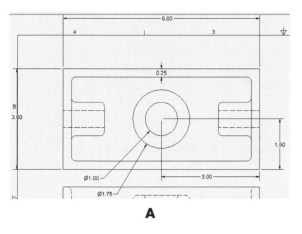 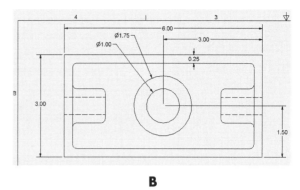

Figure 6.22   Adding and moving model dimensions

Model Dimensions

2.   Move your cursor onto the top view. A red dotted border should appear. Right-click to bring up the context menu and select Get Model Annotations/ Get Model Dimensions. Dimensions from the model should appear on the view, similar to Figure 6.22(a). They are not exactly where you want them to be. Use the cursor to pick and drag the dimensions so that they appear similar to Figure 6.22(b).

Centerlines

3.   Let's add some centerlines. Right-click the top view and pick Automated Centerlines from the context menu. The Centerline Settings dialog appears, similar to Figure 6.23(a). Note which Apply To and Projection buttons are depressed. Pick OK to apply the centerlines. The results should look like Figure 6.23(b). Not all the centerlines you want will appear automatically.

4.   Pick the Drawing Views Panel label and select Drawing Annotation Panel from the drop-down list.

 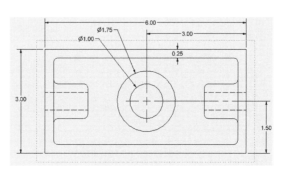

Figure 6.23   Addition of automated centerlines

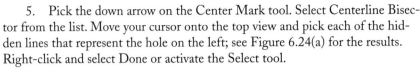

5.   Pick the down arrow on the Center Mark tool. Select Centerline Bisector from the list. Move your cursor onto the top view and pick each of the hidden lines that represent the hole on the left; see Figure 6.24(a) for the results. Right-click and select Done or activate the Select tool.

6.   Adjust the centermarks that are on the center hole so that the extending lines extend over the larger circular feature. This is done by moving your cursor over the centermark until it turns red. Bright green circular marks will appear as well. Move your cursor onto the green circle on the left and pick and drag. Repeat for the other line. See Figure 6.24(b) for the desired results.

Adding Dimensions

7.   Model dimensions placed on a drawing aren't always the way you want them. This is the case with the hole dimension on the top view.

Zoom in on the dimension as shown in Figure 6.25(a). We want it noted that the hole should be all the way through (thru). In this case, you'll delete the model dimension and add a drawing annotation hole note. Pick the dimension and press the Delete key to remove it.

8.   The Drawing Annotation Panel should still be open. If it isn't, open it. Select the Holes/Thread Notes tool and pick the hole in the top view. Using the cursor, drag the hole note into a similar position as on the old model dimension (see Figure 6.25(b)). As you can see, "thru" was added to the note automatically.

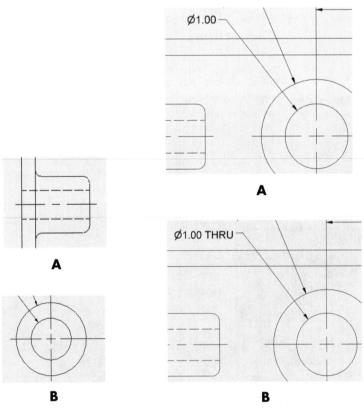

Figure 6.24
Manually adding and adjusting centerlines

Figure 6.25   Deleting a model dimension and adding a hole note

Figure 6.26
Creating a section view
and adding dimensions
and centerlines

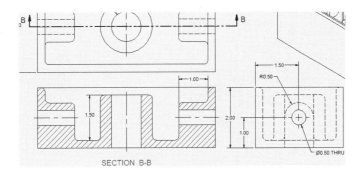

9. Delete the front view and put a section view in its place, using the top view to identify the section line (see Figure 6.26).

10. Use the procedure outlined in Step 2 to add model dimensions to the front and side views. Move them into their proper positions and add any that are missing. Replace the model hole dimension with a hole note. Refer to Figure 6.26 for the completed views.

11. Use the procedure outlined in Steps 3 through 6 to add centerlines to the views (see Figure 6.26).

Section View Hidden Lines

12. Most section views don't have hidden lines shown. Now look at the section view. The right and left inner-curved protrusions appear to be solid from front to back. But in reality there's a gap between the front and rear walls and the protrusions. To help identify this, hidden lines need to be shown on the section view.

To add hidden lines to the section view, right-click the view and select Edit View. When the dialog box appears, pick the Hidden Style button in the lower-right corner of the box. The results should look like Figure 6.27.

Modifying the Model

13. You're now going to modify the model and see its effect on the drawing. Open the part model CBASE but don't close the drawing CBASE.

14. Right-click the hole title (for the small hole) in the browser and select the Edit feature. When the Holes dialog box appears, turn the hole into a tapped hole (see Figure 6.28). Pick OK to apply the change.

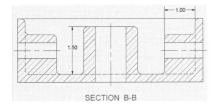

Figure 6.27 Adding hidden lines
to the section view

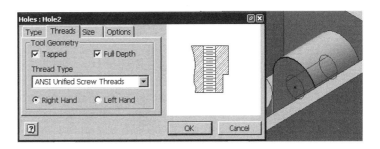

Figure 6.28 Turning a hole into a tapped hole

Figure 6.29
Completed drawing

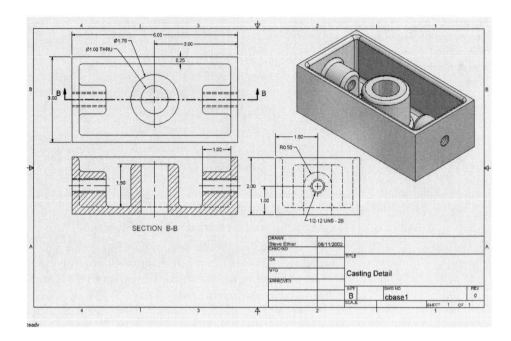

You'll notice that the hole on the other side changed. This is because it was a mirror hole. Anything you do to the original hole is applied to mirrored copy.

15. Save the part model.

16. Return to your drawing of the same part. It may take awhile to complete the drawing on the screen. It has to update from the changes to the part. Watch the browser. You will see some of the view symbols are red, indicating they're being updated. When they turn black again, the update is finished in that view. Observe the small holes. See how they've updated to show the threads. You may have to move the thread note in the side view.

17. The last change to make is to turn the isometric view into a shaded view. Right-click the isometric view and select Edit View from the context menu. When the dialog box appears, pick the Shade Style button and pick OK to complete the change. Your drawing should now look like Figure 6.29.

18. Save your CBASE drawing. Add any other notes you want. You may want to fill the title block in with other text.

In a Nutshell

You're now able to create detailed part drawings from your 3D modeled part. Autodesk Inventor will create your views automatically adding hidden lines, centerlines, and dimensions. As well, various types of section views can be created such as full and half.

To further refine the drawing, you can modify the dimensions by moving them or altering their appearance. You can also add reference dimensions where parametric dimensions are lacking. Dimensions, centerlines, hidden lines, and even edges can be hidden from being displayed to aid in the clarity of the drawing.

The next stage in the learning process is to create assemblies from individual parts. That is coming in the next chapter.

Testing . . . testing . . . 1, 2, 3

Fill-in-the-Blanks

1. There are seven basic view types. They are: _____, _____, _____, _____, _____, _____, and _____.
2. The _____ dialog box contains a list of drawing _____ with one already selected, based on the initial template.
3. A changed dimension affects other features on the part, especially _____. Sometimes when you change a dimension on a part these features will be _____.
4. Annotation dimensions are differentiated from model dimensions on a drawing by allowing you to _____ them where you _____ .
5. Autodesk Inventor does not automatically display _____ dimensions on the drawing, but you can add this information.

True or False

6. Normally, you show hidden lines in section views.   T or F
7. Annotation dimensions are updated automatically when the model is modified.   T or F
8. A project view creates an isometric view from a base view.   T or F
9. You will find that you rarely have to alter the placement of the dimensions to complete the drawing.   T or F

What?

1. What is a base view?

2. Describe the procedure used to move a dimension.

3. Describe the procedure used to hide a dimension.

4. What is the purpose of the Drawing Annotation Panel?

5. Describe the time-saving features that Autodesk Inventor has for generating detail drawings.

6. Under what circumstances would you have to use hidden lines?

7. List and describe each of the seven view types.

 # Let's Get Busy!

1. Create the axle support part shown in Figure 6.30. Once that is done, produce a detail drawing of it similar to Figure 6.30.

   A half section is required. To create a half section view, draw the section line in an L shape as shown in Figure 6.30.

   Use the Edit View tool to display the hidden lines on the section view. You will need to hide various centerlines to clarify the drawing.
2. Create a detail drawing of the lock support part (LOCKSUP) that you created in the Chapter 5 Hands-On. See Figure 6.31 for the layout of the drawing.
3. Create a detail drawing of the collar clamp (CLAMP) modified in Chapter 5, Assignment 1.
4. Create a detail drawing of the pivot joint (PIVOT) that you modified in Chapter 5, Assignment 2.
5. Create a detail drawing of the strap clamp (STRAP) created in Chapter 5, Assignment 4.
6. Create a detail drawing of the die base (DIEBASE) created in Chapter 5, Assignment 5.
7. Create a detail drawing of the miniature pneumatic cylinder body (MINICYL) created in Chapter 5, Assignment 6.

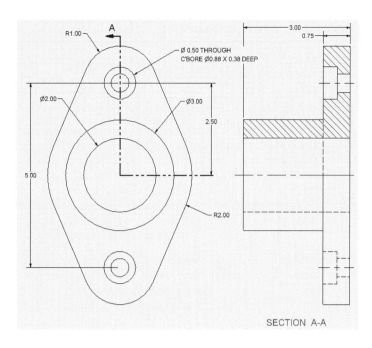

Figure 6.30 Axle support detail drawing

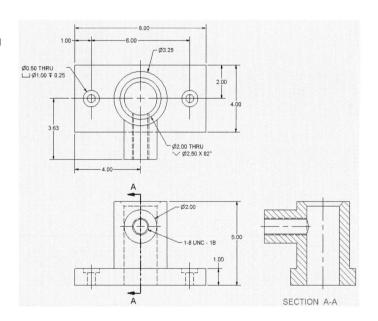

Figure 6.31 Lock support detail drawing

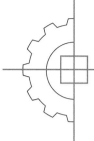

Chapter 7

Assembly Creation

Key Concepts

- Top-down and Bottom-up Assembly Methods
- Placing Components
- Degrees of Freedom
- Part Occurrences
- 3D Assembly Constraints
- Assembly Information
- Weldment Assembly

With Easy to Assemble Instructions . . . No, Really!

The purpose of an assembly is to display a product in its completed form and to illustrate the relationship of its various component parts. Figure 7.1 is, you guessed it, an assembly.

Most often, the ultimate purpose of creating a part is so that it may be fitted into an assembly creating a larger whole. Sometimes an assembly can be very complex and subassemblies are required to break down the larger assembly into smaller, easier to handle packages.

This chapter explains the Autodesk Inventor assembly concepts, the procedure to create an assembly, some editing methods, and design extraction information.

Assembly Concepts

We must first review some Autodesk Inventor assembly concepts before going into the details of creating an assembly. Understanding the approach to creating assemblies will give you a grounding before learning the specifics.

Figure 7.1 An assembly

An assembly file contains a series of individual parts put together in a specific order. The assembly can be created through a top-down approach, a bottom-up approach, or a combination of both.

The purpose of an assembly is to display a product in its completed form and to illustrate the relationship of its various component parts.

Top-down approach   The parts are all created inside the assembly file. This method of assembly creation is useful when you're in the designing stage. You're creating the shapes and sizes of parts as you design.

Bottom-up approach   Each part is created in its own file and referenced into the assembly.

Combination approach   Allows you to maintain an external library of parts while still being able to create a part inside the assembly file as needed.

When part files are placed in the assembly they're added to the Assembly Model browser (see Figure 7.2). Note the first listed part—sgbody:1. It has a pushpin symbol beside it. This signifies that it is a grounded part—it's fixed in its location. Parts you insert afterwards can go anywhere in the assembly unless you make them grounded parts.

Also note the 1 beside the part names. This signifies that it's the first occurrence of the part. It's not the actual part. The actual part remains in its part file. If you insert another occurrence of the part, the number 2 will appear beside the part name. Copies in the assembly environment are called occurrences. You can also place assemblies, referred to as subassemblies.

When the parts are first placed, you're able to move them around anywhere inside the file. The manner in which the part is able to move is referred to as DOF (Degrees Of Freedom). Figure 7.3(a) shows parts in various random positions.

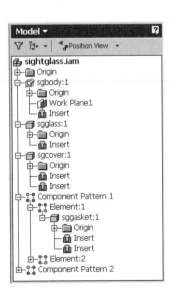

Figure 7.2   Assembly browser

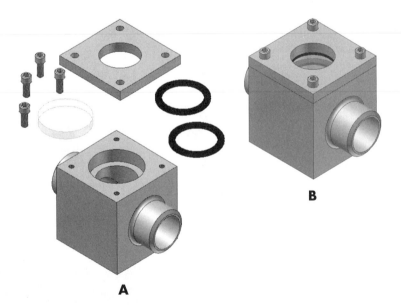

Figure 7.3   Randomly placed parts and in their proper position through Assembly Constraints

To create the assembly, the parts must be placed in their appropriate positions through the use of positional restraints referred to as Assembly Constraints. The Assembly Constraint links parts to each other in specific ways. This controls their DOF in a manner that is instrumental with the application of the part. For instance, if a pin's purpose was to fit into a hole, then the insert Assembly Constraint would be applied to the pin so that it would be positioned into the hole into which it was meant to be inserted. This would restrict its movement. You can apply more than one Assembly Constraint to limit the movement or position of a part. Envision a hinge plate: it can swing back and forth on its hinge pin but cannot move from that pin. In this case, the hinge plate's DOF would be restricted to movement around an axis. Figure 7.3(b) shows the parts constrained to their proper assembled positions. Refer to the browser in Figure 7.2. Look for the label's Insert. It signifies where an Assembly Constraint has been applied to a part.

To aid in the application of constraints, you can use the Move and Rotate tools to move a part to help with its selection. If the part is already constrained, it will move back into its proper position when the assembly is updated or another constraint is applied to the part.

Assembly Options

Before you start creating an assembly, you should review the assembly options just to identify what is already set before an assembly takes place. Open the Options dialog box and open the Assembly tab. You won't need to make any change at this stage.

Creating an Assembly

When you're about to create your assembly, decide what parts you're going to use and the order that you'll assemble them. Autodesk Inventor places these individual parts and subassemblies into an assembly in a hierarchical manner. So it is important to decide at the beginning how the parts are going to go together. By planning at the start, you'll save yourself a lot of headaches and unnecessary work later on. Remember that the first part you create or place is considered the grounded part. All other parts are placed based on this part.

Like most of the procedures in Autodesk Inventor, to start an assembly you make use of a template file using the New command. You can recognize the template by its icon which is three blocks assembled together. During the assembly process you can place or create subassemblies. You'll be able to recognize them by the addition of an assembly icon in the browser. Once you've selected a template file, the screen switches to the assembly environment. An Assembly Panel similar to Figure 7.4 will appear.

Figure 7.4
Assembly Panel

External Part Libraries

Create separate file folders/directories for categories of parts that you create that you will want to use over again. For example, create a folder that contains different types of fasteners such as nuts and bolts.

Placing a Component

The procedure to add parts to the assembly from outside part files is to use the Place Component tool. An Open dialog box appears that is similar to Figure 7.5, which shows a list of parts and assemblies in the current workgroup. You can also use the Look in: list to change locations.

From the list you select the part or assembly you want to add to the assembly. If you select an assembly, it will become a subassembly in the new assembly. The first placement, whether part or assembly, becomes a grounded component—fixed in its location. Any other parts or assemblies placed can be located anywhere and then constrained to their proper positions. When done, press the ESC key—or right-click and select Done from the context menu.

Creating a Component

You can also create parts "on-the-fly" during an assembly creation. When you select the Create Component, the Create In-Place Component dialog box appears as shown in Fig-

Drag and Drop Components

You can drag and drop components from the browser. Just pick and drag the name in the browser onto the graphics screen and an occurrence will appear, ready to be placed into position.

If you have multiple files open, you can drag from one file's browser to the other file's graphics window. Note that both files' graphics windows have to be displayed. This is done from the Window pull-down menu.

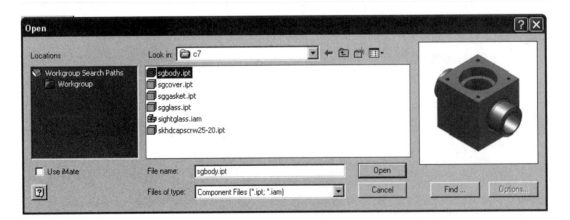

Figure 7.5   Open dialog box

Figure 7.6 Create In-Place Component dialog and semi-transparent assembly

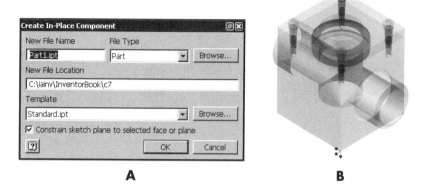

A   **B**

ure 7.6(a). The various settings, such as part file name, location, and template, are selected. When you select OK, you're prompted to pick a surface to use as the sketch plane. Once that's done, the assembly will become semitransparent to make it easier to sketch as shown in Figure 7.6(b). You can then create a part as usual from the base sketch.

Patterning a Component

The Pattern Component tool allows you to create patterned copies of a part. It operates in a similar fashion to patterning sketch objects or sketch features when creating a part. You can also edit the pattern afterward by right-clicking on the component pattern name in the browser and selecting Edit. Figure 7.7 shows the browser, Edit Component Pattern dialog box, and the patterned components.

Part Occurrence

When you add parts to your assembly, they are placed in the assembly as an occurrence. Figure 7.8 shows multiple occurrences of a socket head cap screw. If you change the original part, the associated occurrences will change automatically. If you change an external part, the occurrence will change as soon as the assembly is opened. With an external part, all the information such as its name and attributes is stored in the original drawing file where the part was created. The occurrences are only copies of the original.

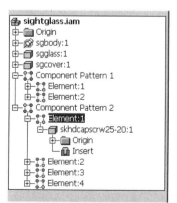
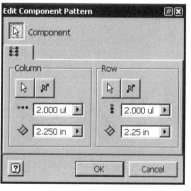

Figure 7.7   Patterned Components

Figure 7.8   Part
occurrences

Placement of Parts/Occurrence

It doesn't matter where you place the instances to start with in the assembly. They can be moved anywhere until the Assembly constraints are added. Once the Assembly constraints are added, the part's placement is controlled. You can still move the parts using the standard MOVE command but as soon as a constraint is added, the part will automatically move back to its constrained position.

Assembly Constraints

Once the parts have been placed, you need to control placement or restrict their movement using Assembly Constraints. This is accomplished by using the Place Constraint tool. When you select the tool, a Place Constraint dialog box similar to Figure 7.9 will appear. There are four constraints: mate, tangent, angle, and insert. You can apply more than one constraint to a part. This can effectively control its placement.

With every constraint you need to select two sets of geometry: first set and second set. This selection controls how the two parts will be linked. There are four types of geometry sets: edge, point, axis, and surface. Which ones you're able to use depends on the geometry of the part and the type of constraint you're using. Figure 7.10 shows some of the selection geometry.

To see which type of selection is possible on a part, move your cursor over the desired area and the various geometry will be highlighted. Note that if you pause at a location, such as a linear edge, the selection cycle tool appears. This allows you to cycle through the possible geometry, to select an edge or a point where two edges intersect.

If you move your cursor near a linear edge of the part, the edge will be highlighted. If the edge is circular, the center point may be highlighted (see Figure 7.10(a)).

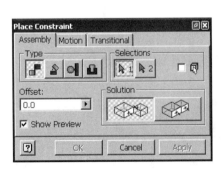

Figure 7.9   Place Constraint
dialog box

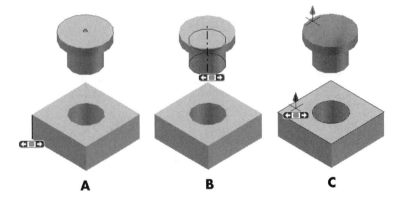

Figure 7.10   Selection geometry

If you move your cursor near a curved surface, the axes will be highlighted (see Figure 7.10(b)).

If you move your cursor near a flat surface, the surface will be highlighted. Note the surface symbol. The point where you pick on the surface will be used as the location point on the surface (see Figure 7.10(c)).

You also have the option of changing the set type after picking. Usually you try to pick the same type for the first and second sets.

After you have picked the geometry sets, you can enter an offset distance. This allows you to enter a value that will cause the geometry sets to be spaced apart or overlap each other. Sometimes there's more than one solution to a constraint. There are solution tools to allow you to decide which solution to use.

Figures 7.11 through 7.14 show the application of the different Assembly constraints. The "before" image shows the parts with the geometry sets selected and the "after" image shows the results of the constraint. Refer to these figures and the following text describing the different Assembly constraints.

 Mate The Mate constraint can be considered the all-purpose constraint used to position a part in reference to another part. You can apply more than one Mate constraint to shift the part into position (see Figure 7.11).

 Tangent The Tangent constraint can be used when you want to line up one part with another using tangent points on each part's surface (see Figure 7.12).

 Angle The Angle constraint is used when you want a specific angle from one part to another (see Figure 7.13). This constraint can be useful when you want one part to pivot a number of degrees from another part.

 Insert The Insert constraint is used when you want to align two circular features with each other (see Figure 7.14). It is not necessary that they're inserted into each other. For example, you may have two parts with holes that must line up with each other.

Figure 7.11
Application of Mate constraint

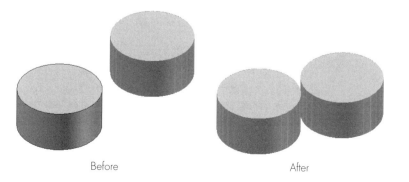

Figure 7.12
Application of Tangent constraint

Figure 7.13
Application of Angle
constraint

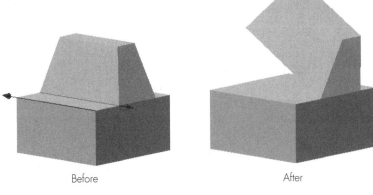

Before   After

Figure 7.14
Application of Insert
Assembly constraint

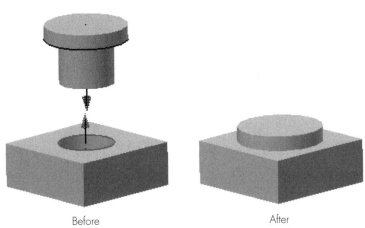

Before   After

Applying Assembly Constraints

You can apply more than one constraint to a part to control its placement. Don't be alarmed when a part moves into an unusual position when a constraint is applied. It usually means that you need to apply another constraint to control it further. Remember, you can always delete a constraint and reapply it if the results aren't satisfactory.

Advanced Assembly Constraints

There are two more assembly constraints that are more advanced than the other four. These are Motion and Transitional. Motion is used to apply movement of one part to another. Transitional is used to control the movement of one part's surface (usually circular) to another part's surface (usually flat) such as a cylinder rolling inside a flat slot.

Degrees of Freedom

When you first place a part, before you apply Assembly constraints, it has unlimited degrees of freedom (DOF). This means that the part can move anywhere in the assembly. When you start applying Assembly constraints, you're limiting the part's DOF. Different constraints limit DOF differently.

You can display the DOF for any part by highlighting it in the browser and right-clicking. Select Properties from the context menu and open the Occurrence tab. Under

Figure 7.15
Degrees of freedom
displayed before and
after part is constrained

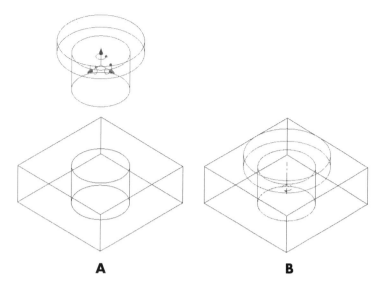

A   **B**

Moving Parts

If you pick on a constrained part and try to move it by dragging, it will only move based on its DOF. If you want to change the location of a part because of obstruction during assembly, the Move and Rotate tools will allow you to relocate parts. However, these commands have no effect on applied Assembly constraints. If you update the assembly, the part will return to its constrained position.

the Properties section there is a Degrees of Freedom box. When it's checked, a DOF symbol appears on the part (see Figure 7.15(a)). The DOF icon is displayed for the pin. It has unlimited movement capabilities. Now see Figure 7.15(b). The Insert constraint has been applied. The pin's DOF is now limited to revolution only. Look closely at the center of the pin and you'll see an axis line and a small semicircle with an arrow on the end. This is the current state of the DOF symbol.

Editing Assembly Constraints

You can edit or delete an assembly constraint after it has been applied. If you delete a constraint, the part's position will not change. You can use the browser to edit or delete a constraint. If you double-click the constraint, the Edit Dimension dialog box will appear allowing you to change the constraint offset distance. If you right-click on the constraint, you can select from the context menu to edit or delete.

Hands-On: Creating Assemblies

In this exercise, you're going to create an assembly. The assembly will use the bottom-up method with all the parts already created outside the assembly file.

1.   Start a new assembly drawing using the Standard (in).iam template. Figure 7.16 shows what the completed assembly will look like.

Figure 7.16
Completed joint
assembly

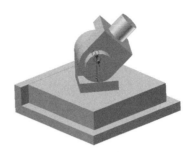

2.   Use the Place Component tool to place the pivot-base.ipt. Figure 7.17 shows the Open dialog box with the part file highlighted. Since it's the first part to be placed, it will be placed automatically as a grounded part.

3.   Zoom out to give you more space and use the Place Component tool again to place the following components: pivot-joint, pivot-pin, and pivot-plate. Figure 7.18 shows the random placement. Note that the pivot-joint will be used twice, so it's required to be placed twice.

4.   Right-click the pivot-joint:1 name in the browser and pick Properties from the context menu. Open the Occurrence tab in the Properties dialog box and turn on (check) the Degrees of Freedom box. Pick Apply and then OK to

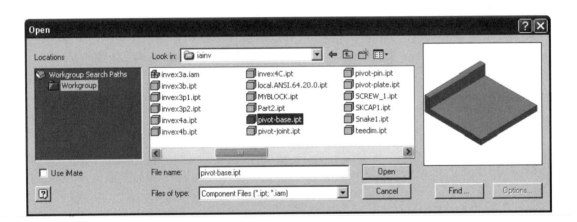

Figure 7.17   Open dialog box with pivot-base.ipt highlighted

Figure 7.18   Parts
randomly arranged

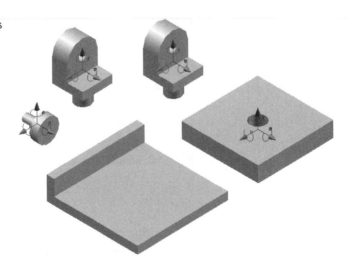

exit the dialog box. The Degrees of Freedom symbol will appear on the part. Repeat this for all the parts.

Observe the DOF for each part. All of them, except one, have total freedom of movement. The joint-base part has no freedom of movement. It is the first part in the assembly hierarchy and is referred to as the grounded part. All the other parts' positions will be based on it.

5.   Now it's time to apply the various Assembly constraints. Pick Place Constraint to display the Place Constraint dialog box.

6.   When applying constraints, apply them to the parts in the order you want them to be assembled. In this case, the joint-plate with the hole in it will be constrained to the joint-base. This will involve the application of the Mate constraint three times.

Select the Mate tool and pick the bottom face of the joint-plate as shown in Figure 7.19(a) and accept it when you have the correct face and correct arrow direction picked. Then, pick the top face of the joint-base as shown in Figure 7.19(b) and accept it when you have the correct face and correct arrow direction picked. Review the dialog box shown in Figure 7.20. The offset is set to 0, so that the two faces will touch and the Solution tool is set to Mate. Pick Apply and the results will look similar to Figure 7.20. Your assembly may look different depending on where you picked on the parts. Note the DOF for the joint-plate. It has lost the Z-axis movement because of the Mate constraint.

Select the Mate tool again and pick the left face of the joint-plate as shown in Figure 7.21 and accept it when you have the correct face and correct arrow direction picked. Then, pick the left face of the joint-base as shown in Figure 7.21 and accept it when you have the correct face and correct arrow direction picked. Enter 0.5 for the offset distance. The joint-plate part moved until its side face was 0.5 away from the side face of the joint-base. Note the DOF for the joint-plate. It has lost the Y-axis movement degree of freedom because of the

Figure 7.19
Applying the first Mate constraint

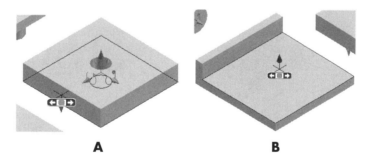

A   **B**

Figure 7.20   Place Constraint dialog box and the mated parts

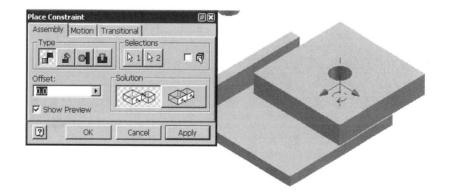

Figure 7.21
Applying the second
Mate constraint

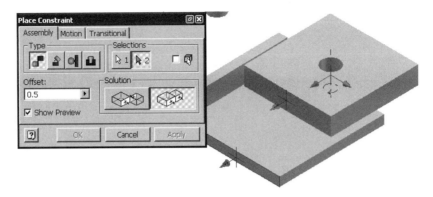

second Mate constraint. Don't forget to set the Solution to Flush and pick the
Apply button.

Select the Mate tool again and pick the rear face of the joint-plate as shown
in Figure 7.22(a) and accept it when you have the correct face and correct arrow
direction picked. Then, pick the face of the joint-base as shown in Figure 7.22(b)
and again accept it when you have the correct face and correct arrow direction
picked. Enter 0 for the offset distance. Remember to use the Mate solution tool
and to pick Apply. The joint-plate part moved until its rear face touched the face
of the joint-base. Note the DOF for the joint-plate. It has lost all its DOF.

7.   The next part to constrain is one of the joint-pivot parts. You're going
to insert it into the hole in the joint-plate.

Select the Insert tool and select the circle base of the cylinder (not the end)
of the joint-pivot as shown in Figure 7.23(a) and accept it when the arrow direction is correct. You'll have to use the Free Rotate tool to display the underside of
the joint-pivot. Next, pick the top circle of the hole in the joint-plate as shown

Figure 7.22
Applying the third Mate
constraint

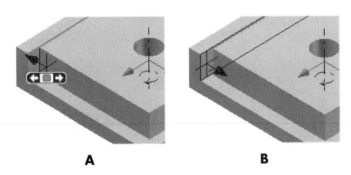

A   B

Figure 7.23
Applying the first Insert
constraint

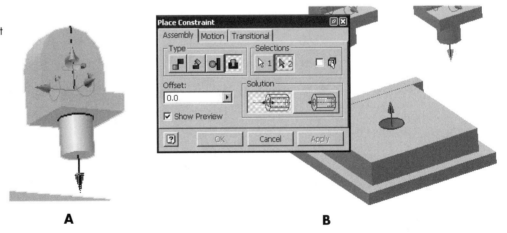

A   B

in Figure 7.23(b) and accept it when the arrow direction is correct. Enter 0 for the offset distance. The joint-pivot should have moved so that its cylinder is inserted into the hole. Don't forget to pick the Apply button before continuing.

8.   The next part to constrain is a second joint-pivot part. You're going to use an Insert constraint to align it with the hole in the other joint-pivot.

Select the Insert tool and select the top circle of the hole of the second joint-pivot as shown in Figure 7.24. Accept it when the arrow direction is correct. Next, pick the front circle of the hole in the first joint-pivot as shown in Figure 7.24 and accept it when the arrow direction is correct. Enter 0 for the offset distance. The second joint-pivot should have moved so that its hole aligns with the hole of the first joint-pivot. The second joint-pivot overlaps the first joint-pivot. You'll fix that soon.

9.   Now you're going to insert the joint-pin into the hole.

Select the Insert tool and select the base circle (not the end) of joint-pin as shown in Figure 7.25. Accept it when the arrow direction is correct. Next, pick the front circle of the hole in the second joint-pivot as shown in Figure 7.25 and accept it when the arrow direction is correct. Enter 0 for the offset distance. The joint-pin should have moved so that it is inserted into the hole.

Figure 7.24
Applying the second Insert constraint

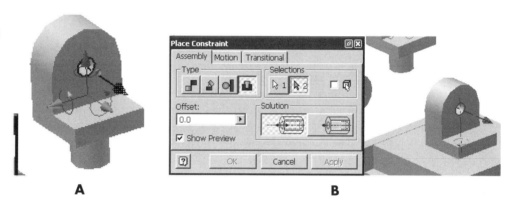

A   B

Figure 7.25
Applying the third Insert constraint

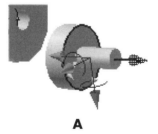

A

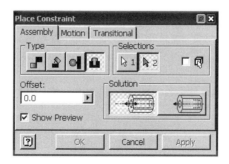

B

Figure 7.26
Displaying a shaded
view of the assembly

10. Close the Place Constraints dialog box. Pick and drag on the right-most joint-pivot. Move your cursor around the screen and see what happens. The parts move but only based on their degrees of freedom. Move the cursor so that the assembly looks similar to Figure 7.26.

11. Save your new assembly as FlexJoint.asm.

Assembly Information

There are three types of information retrieval that can be performed from an assembly: checking for interference, checking minimum 3D distance, and retrieving mass property information.

 First, you can check for any interference between two assembled parts. To do this, select Analyze Interference from the Tools pull-down menu. You can check nested parts or subassemblies. To do this, select two sets of parts or subassemblies and the command will identify the interference (see Figure 7.27).

Standard Parts

Standard parts such as nuts and bolts can be dragged and dropped into your assembly by using the Library browser. If you pick the Model label in the browser, you'll have a choice of the Model browser or the Library browser. The content is provided by Library servers that are either local (residing in your computer) or are accessed using the network (local network or the Web). The Library is a separate installation from Autodesk Inventor. You may have to activate i-drop translator from the Add-in-Manager. This is located in the Windows Start menu: Programs/Inventor/Tools folder.

Figure 7.27
Interference Analysis
dialog box

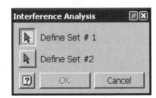

Figure 7.28
Retrieving mass
property information

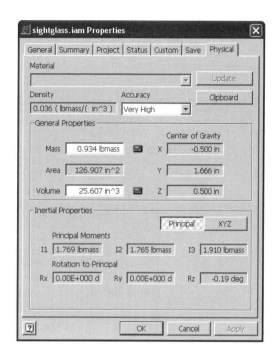

You can check for the minimum Assembly distance between two sets of parts by selecting Measure Distance from the Tools pull-down menu. Once you have selected the two sets of parts, the minimum distance between the parts will be given.

Also, you can retrieve mass property information such as mass, volume, and center of gravity. To do this, right-click the assembly name in the browser and select Properties from the context menu (see Figure 7.28). Open the Physical tab. Once you have selected the part, a dialog box similar to Figure 7.28 is presented.

Weldment Assembly

Weldment assembly design is an extension of the assembly modeling environment. In assembly weldments, you create assemblies as you normally do but add weld symbols and fillet weld objects. These symbols and objects can be automatically added to a drawing. To start a weldment, Select New from the File pull-down menu and open a weldment template. You'll then be presented with the weldment assembly environment.

In a Nutshell

Creating assemblies is the logical culmination of your part creation. There are various methods of assembling parts by applying assembly constraints. These constraints limit a part's degrees of freedom so that the part moves in a way appropriate with its purpose in the assembly. Once you have the parts assembled, you can extract information such as interference between parts or mass properties.

The next stage is to create assembly drawings from your assembly. This involves creating scenes and is explained in the next chapter.

Testing . . . testing . . . 1, 2, 3

Matching

1. Draw lines connecting the approach in the first column to the characteristics that define it in the second column.

1st column   **2nd column**

a. Top-down approach   parts are all created inside the assembly file

b. Bottom-up approach   maintains an external library of parts

c. Combination approach   part is created in its own file

Fill-in-the-Blanks

2. The parts are first listed inside a(n) _____.

3. A copy of a part is also known as a(n) _____.

4. Remember: The first part you create or externally attach is considered the _____.

5. There are four constraints: _____, _____, _____, and _____.

6. There are three types of information retrieval that can be performed from an assembly:
    1. _____
    2. _____
    3. _____

True or False

7. You can recognize the assembly template by its icon, which is four blocks assembled together.   T or F

8. The Move and Rotate tools allow you to permanently relocate parts.   T or F

Multiple Choice

9. DOF stands for
    a. degree of focus.
    b. decrees of fraternity.
    c. danger of falling.
    d. degrees of freedom.

10. The assembly becomes semi-transparent when a(n)
    a. sketch plane is applied.
    b. work plane is applied.
    c. part is applied.
    d. assembly is deleted.

12. If you change the original part, the associated occurrences will change
    a. but not in your lifetime.
    b. automatically.
    c. as soon as the assembly is opened.
    d. when you use the Update tool.

What?

1. List and explain the three types of information retrieval that can be performed from an assembly.

2. What is the purpose of an Assembly constraint?

3. List and define the four types of Assembly constraints.

4. What are the differences between a top-down approach and a bottom-up approach?

5. Imagine a simple, mechanical tool that you have used. Explain two of the constraints that would need to be applied to ensure its proper functioning.

6. With every constraint you need to select two sets of geometry: the first set and second set. Why?

Let's Get Busy!

1. Start a new assembly file and assemble the parts contained in the iainv/SGLASS directory to create the sight glass assembly shown in Figure 7.29.

   The exploded view is shown to help explain how the parts go together. Do *not* create an exploded assembly for this assignment.

   A sight glass is used so that liquid flowing through a pipe can be observed. The following is a list of the parts:

SGBODY	This is the main body and should be attached first.
SGGASKET	The gasket should be attached next. Two instances are required.

Figure 7.29   Sight
glass assembly

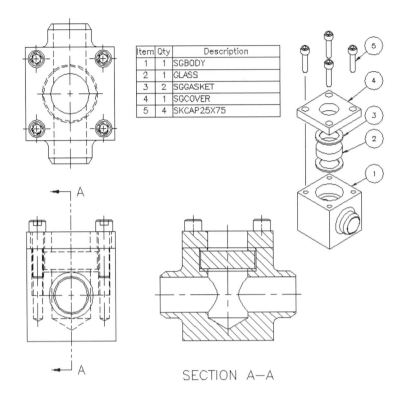

Item	Qty	Description
1	1	SGBODY
2	1	GLASS
3	2	SGGASKET
4	1	SGCOVER
5	4	SKCAP25X75

SECTION A—A

SGGLASS	This part is a piece of circular glass that goes between the two gaskets.
SGCOVER	The cover holds the gaskets and glass in place.
skhdcapscrw25-20	This is a socket head cap screw that is 1/4 diameter by 3/4 long. You need four of them to hold the cover in place.

2. Start a new assembly file and assemble the parts contained in the iainv/ VBLOCK directory to create the Vblock assembly shown in Figure 7.30.

The exploded view is shown to help explain how the parts go together. Do *not* create an exploded assembly for this assignment.

A Vblock assembly is used to restrict the movement of a cylindrical piece so that it can be worked on. You clamp the cylindrical piece between the edges of the VBLOCK and the PLATE on the SCREW.

The following is a list of the parts:

VB-BODY	This is the main part and should be the grounded part (attached first).
VB-CLAMP	This part slides into the side slots in the VBLOCK.
VB-SCREW	The screw threads into the clamp.
VB-HANDLE	The handle slides into the hole in the head of the screw.
VB-BALL	The ball fits on the end of the handle to stop it from sliding off.
VB-PLATE	The plate sits on the bottom of the screw.
VB-SKCAP	The socket head cap screw fits into the plate and secures it to the bottom of the screw.

Figure 7.30 Vblock assembly

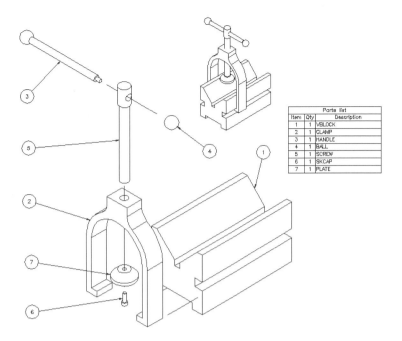

Parts list		
Item	Qty	Description
1	1	VBLOCK
2	1	CLAMP
3	1	HANDLE
4	1	BALL
5	1	SCREW
6	1	SKCAP
7	1	PLATE

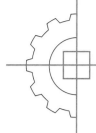

Chapter 8

Assembly Drawing

Key Concepts

◆ Assembly Presentations
◆ Exploded Parts and Tweaking
◆ Precise View Rotation
◆ Animation
◆ Drawing Standard
◆ Bill of Materials
◆ Parts List and Part Balloons

Show and Tell

Once you have created an assembly, you'll normally want to show it to others in the form of an assembly drawing. The assembly drawing can display the assembly in different forms such as exploded or sectioned. You can identify all the parts using part balloons and list them inside a parts list. Figure 8.1 shows an assembly drawing.

This chapter explains the procedure used to create a presentation view, to arrange assembly views, to add part balloons, and to create a parts list.

Figure 8.1
Assembly drawing

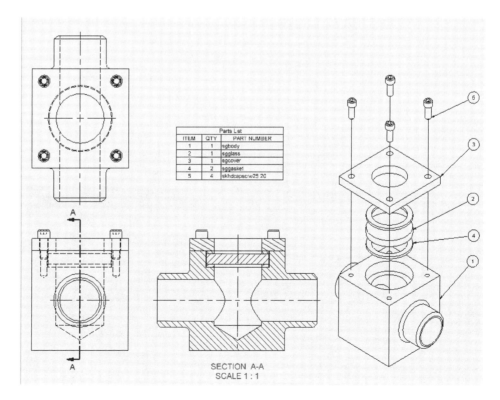

Assembly Presentations

Assembly views are used to display the assembly in different ways without altering the assembly model constraints. In a view, you can change the viewpoint, separate the parts for clarification, and add assembly trails to show how the parts are assembled. You can create as many different views as required to help describe the assembly. Once this is done, you'll place or use the different views to create the assembly drawing.

Standard.ipn

To start creating views, select Standard.ipn from the New file dialog box under the English tab. The Presentation environment will appear with its own Panel and Browser.

New View

To create a new view, select the Create View tool and the Select Assembly dialog box will appear. If you already have an assembly open, it will default to it. You can use the Explore Directories button to locate any assembly file (see Figure 8.2). Once you've selected the assembly file, you need to select a design view and whether to use a manual explosion or an automatic explosion. Explosions are used to separate the assembly parts for clarification. When you pick the OK button, a view of the assembly will appear.

**Assembly views are used to display
the assembly in different ways without
altering the assembly model constraints.**

The explosion distance is the distance the parts will be initially separated by in the scene. You can enter a value of 0 so that the parts remain in their place or enter a value greater than 0 to separate them. The direction the parts move depends on the number of constraints applied to the part. If there is more than one constraint applied to a part it may not move and remain stationary. You can alter the explosion factor for individual parts after the view is created.

Explosion Factor

The overall explosion factor is useful when all the parts line up along one axis. We recommend leaving the explosion factor value at 0 for assemblies that use a variety of axes. This will give you more control over moving the parts later on.

Figure 8.2   Select Assembly dialog box

Tweaking Parts

Tweaking is the term Autodesk Inventor uses to describe the action of moving the parts in a scene. The purpose is to create exploded views or to alter the position of parts for clarity in different views. One important item to note: A tweak can be edited. If you want to change a tweak, you can highlight the tweak name in the Browser for a particular part. A value box will appear at the bottom of the browser allowing you to change the tweak distance or angle. You can apply more that one tweak to a part to get it into position. Figure 8.3 shows an assembly with tweaks applied. Note the line extending from the cap screw to the body. This is referred to as a trail and is used to indicate the intended travel of the part to its assembled position. Figure 8.4 shows the linear and rotational types of tweaks.

One important item to note: A tweak can be edited.

To apply a tweak, use the Tweak Component tool or right-click on the part name in the browser. The Tweak Component dialog box is used to apply the tweak to one or more parts that you select. Refer to Figure 8.3 and the following descriptions.

Figure 8.3
Exploded assembly using tweaks with trails added and the Tweak Component dialog box

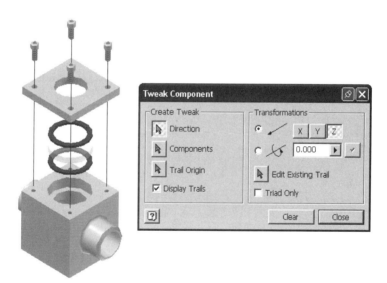

Figure 8.4   Applying the two types of tweaks

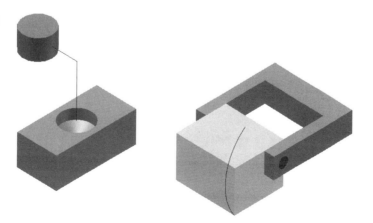

Quick Tweak Modifications

Highlight the tweak in the browser or on the graphics screen. You'll notice a green node appear at the end of the tweak line. If you pick and drag on the node, you can adjust the tweak dynamically. If you right-click to bring up the context menu, you can delete, edit, or change the visibility of a tweak.

Create Tweak Section

Direction	Used to identify the direction for a linear move or the axis for rotation. Once you pick the button, then select an edge, face, or feature on any component.
Components	Used to select the part or parts to be tweaked. You can select them in the graphics window or the browser.
Trail Origin	Used to set the start point of the trail. The trail is an identifying line that extends along the path of the move or rotation tweak. If you don't specify the origin, it's placed at the center of mass of the part.
Display Trails	Used to display or hide the trail identifier lines.

Transformation Section

Linear	When used, select a linear direction axis, enter a distance, and click Apply.
Rotational	When used, select a rotation axis, enter the degrees of rotation, and click Apply.
Linear Direction	Once a linear axis is selected, you can change the linear direction.

Value Box	Enter the linear distance or the degrees of rotation depending on the type of transformation.
Create Tweak	Creates the tweak based on the settings.
Edit Existing Trail	Used to initiate the Edit mode of existing tweaks. Once turned on, you can select existing tweaks and make adjustments.
Triad Only	Used to rotate the triad (XYZ axes symbol) without moving the parts. This is used to determine the orientation of the triad before applying a linear or rotational transformation. This can be helpful when moving a part at an angle other than the linear axes of existing parts.
Clear	Used to clear any previous settings before starting a new tweak.

Precise View Rotation

When you want an exact view orientation of your assembly you can use the Precise View Rotation tool. Figure 8.5 shows the Incremental View Rotate dialog box. By setting an incremental value and using the various rotation buttons, you can generate the exact view that you're looking for.

Figure 8.5
Incremental View Rotate
dialog box

Picking Reference Geometry

You can use any part as the reference geometry for a tweak. It doesn't even have to be on the part you are tweaking. The edge of the part you pick to tweak is used as the axis and controls the direction of travel. Try different edges until the travel axis is aligned to the desired direction.

Animation

You can generate animated views of your tweaked assembly. Selecting the Animate tool presents you with the Animation dialog box shown in Figure 8.6. Reviewing the dialog box, you'll see buttons similar to a VCR control.

If you pick the Play button, the screen will display an animated view of the application of the assembly tweaks.

There is also a Record button that you can use to record an AVI file (Figure 8.7(a)) and various compression types (Figure 8.7(b)). The easiest compressor to use is Full Frames (uncompressed). It generates the largest file but it's also the clearest. When the video is recorded, you can use an AVI player such as Windows Media Player to view the video outside the Autodesk Inventor program.

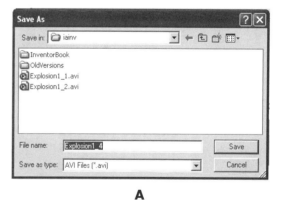

A

Figure 8.6   Animation dialog box

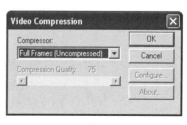

B

Figure 8.7   Save As and Video Compression
dialog boxes

Hands-On: Creating a Presentation View

In this exercise you'll create a Presentation View using parts already assembled. You'll tweak the parts to get them into an exploded position and display their assembly trails.

1. Open file iainvex8A.iam. The model shows two assembly groups. You'll apply different tweaks to each one.

Creating the Presentation View

2. Use the New tool and open the English standard.ipn presentation template. The Presentation environment is then opened.

3. Select the Create View tool. The Select Assembly dialog box appears as shown in Figure 8.8. Since you have already opened the assembly file, it appears in the file window. We're going to start with the default view and leave it at the manual explosion method. When you pick the OK button, the view of the assembly will appear.

Assembly trails are used to indicate the travel of a part from its exploded or tweaked position to its assembled position.

Adding Linear Tweaks

4. Highlight the presentation name in the browser and right-click. Select Expand All Children so that you can see all the parts in the browser.

5. Select the Tweak Components tool and the Tweak Component dialog box appears, as shown in Figure 8.8. With the Direction tool depressed move your cursor over the bronze-shaded pin that is on the left assembly. Pause on the edge of the pin and the triad (XYZ axes) symbol will appear in the center of the pin as shown in Figure 8.9. Note that the Z axis is pointing upward. Pick that location.

Figure 8.8 Select Assembly dialog box

Figure 8.9   Tweak
Component dialog box
and selected linear
direction

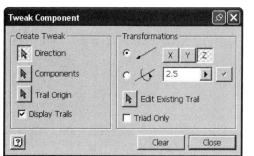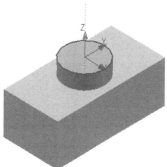

The Components button is now depressed. Select the pin in the graphics window. Figure 8.9 shows the various settings. Note that the Linear transform button is active and enter a value of 2.5 for the distance the part will be moved.

Once you've adjusted your settings, pick the Apply checkmark tool and the tweak will be applied. The pin should move upwards by 2.5 inches. The results should look similar to Figure 8.10(a). Do *not* close the dialog box.

Pick the Clear tool to reset the tweak settings. Pick the Direction tool and select the same location on the pin as before.

Using the Components tool, select the pin again. Make sure that the Linear Tweak button is active. This time, depress the X axis button so that the direction of the tweak is going to go along the X axis.

Enter a value of -2.0 for the tweak distance and pick the Apply tool. The results should look similar to Figure 8.10(b).

6.   Close the dialog box and save your presentation file as ex8a.ipn.

Adding a Rotational Tweak

7.   Select the Tweak Components tool and make sure that the Rotation transform is active. Using the Direction tool, select the edge of the small bronze shaft on the right assembly (see Figure 8.11).

Use the Components tool to select the large swing block on the right assembly.

Figure 8.10
Applying linear tweaks

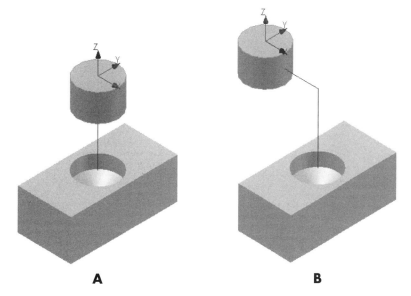

A   B

Figure 8.11 Tweak Component dialog box and selected rotational direction

Figure 8.12 Applying rotational tweak

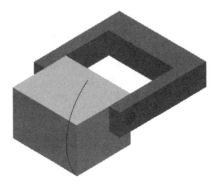

Use the Trail Origin tool to pick the block's upper corner, closest to the viewer. This will set where the trail will start.

Figure 8.11 shows the various settings. Note that the Rotational transform button is active and enter a value of 90 for the degrees the part will rotate.

Once you have adjusted your settings, pick the Apply checkmark tool and the tweak will be applied. The block should rotate 90 degrees. The results should look similar to Figure 8.12.

8. Save your presentation file as ex8A.

View Animated Tweaks

9. In this step, you're going to animate the tweaks. First, Zoom All so that you can see both assemblies.

10. Select the Animate tool and the Animation dialog box will appear.

11. Click the Play button and watch how the parts are animated.

12. Click the Play Reverse button and the animation goes in reverse. Experiment with the other buttons.

13. Use the Record button to create an AVI file called Presentation1. Remember to use Full Compression. Once the Record button is active, click the Play button to record the animation.

Use Windows Explorer to find the AVI file in your directory and double-click on it. The Windows Media Player should appear and play your animation.

Applying View Presentation

You're going to apply what you have learned to create two presentation views from an assembly already created.

Figure 8.13 Bolt assembly used for presentation view

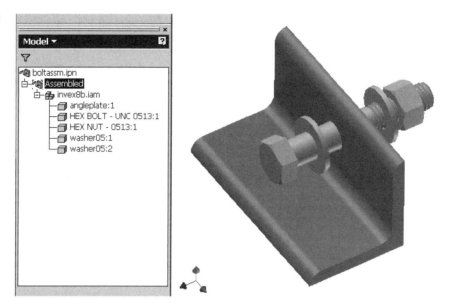

Figure 8.14 Exploded view

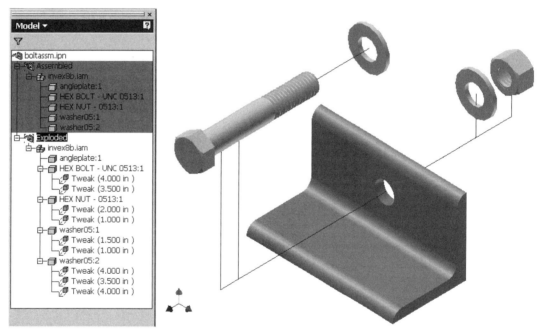

1. Open file iainvex8B. It contains a bolt, a nut, and two washers. They have been assembled onto an angle bracket. Figure 8.13 shows the assembly.

2. You're going to create two presentation views. The first presentation view, to be called Assembled, shows the parts in their assembled positions (see Figure 8.13). The second presentation view, to be called Exploded, shows the parts in exploded positions (see Figure 8.14).

Proceed to create the two presentation views. Then use various tweaks to get the parts into their positions. Add trails to the exploded parts.

3. Save your files as BOLTASSM. You're going to use it in the next Hands-On.

4. Generate an animated AVI file showing the assembly of the exploded view.

Creating Assembly Views

The procedure to create assembly views is similar to the manner in which you create part views in a drawing. The only difference is that you can make use of presentation views so that you can show the assembly in its different stages of assembly.

To add an assembly presentation view, enter into a drawing file (new or previously created) and pick the Base View tool. You will be presented with a dialog box as shown in Figure 8.15. Note the File name is set to an *.ipn* instead of an *.ipt*. This is because you're inserting a presentation view instead of a part view. To select a presentation file, use the Explore Directories tool and remember to set the file type to ipn. Also note the Presentation View name. You can select from a list of views created in the presentation file.

Once you have picked the presentation file and the presentation view, you can add the view to the drawing in the same manner as you did with individual parts. You must create a base view first. Afterward, you can create section assembly views. Figure 8.16 shows an assembly drawing.

Figure 8.15
Drawing View dialog box showing a presentation file and presentation view

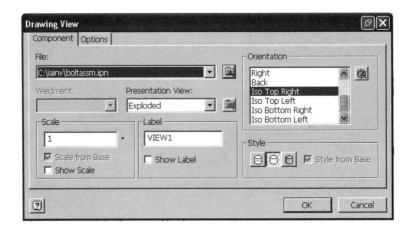

Figure 8.16   Layout showing presentation views created from views, exploded and nonexploded

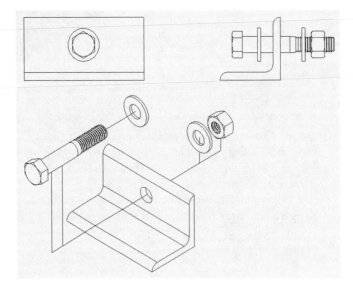

Creating Views from Presentation Views

To create views from different presentation views in the same drawing, you need to create a base view for each presentation file. From the base view, you can create other views such as isometric or section. Once this is done, you can delete the base view while retaining the other views.

Parts List

Once you've created and laid out your assembly views, the next step is to add a parts list to the assembly drawing. As its name implies, this is a list of the parts used in the assembly, as well as other information such as quantity and material used. Figure 8.17 shows a typical bill of materials. The layout and settings for a parts list are determined by the settings in the active drafting standard. However, once a parts list is placed, you modify it in any way for that drawing.

Drafting Standards

The drafting standard used is set by the template used to initially create the file. To see what the drafting standards are for the parts list, open the Part List tab of the Drafting Standard dialog box (see Figure 8.18(a)). To access the dialog box, select Standards from the Format pull-down menu.

From the Parts List tab, you can control every aspect, such as text style, sorting order, the title of the list, and others. There is also a Balloon tab used to select the type of part balloons to be used (see Figure 8.18(b)).

Adding a Parts List

To add a parts list to your drawing, select the Parts List tool from the Drawing Annotation Panel. You then are prompted to select a view to generate the list of parts. When you've picked a view, the Parts List - Item Numbering dialog box appears, similar to Figure 8.19(a). This dialog box is used to make some adjustments before the parts list is placed on the drawing. A rectangular object representing the parts list will appear, attached to the cursor. Place the rectangle where you want the parts list to go.

Figure 8.17
Assembly with parts list

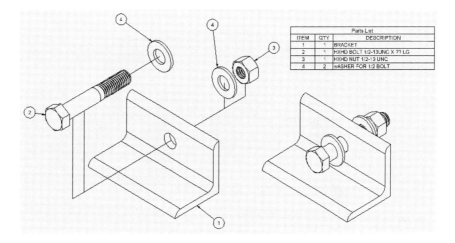

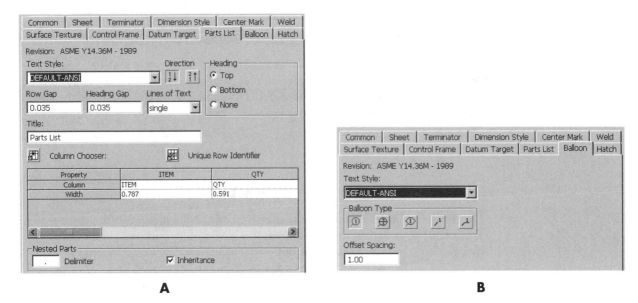

Figure 8.18   Partial Parts List tab and partial Balloon tab of the
Drafting Standards dialog box

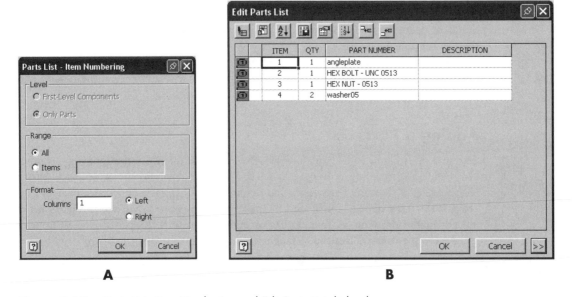

Figure 8.19   Parts List - Item Numbering and Edit Parts List dialog boxes

To edit the parts list, move your cursor over it and right-click. From the context menu, select Edit Parts List. The Edit Parts List dialog box will appear as shown in Figure 8.19(b). Using this dialog box you can make any changes you want to the parts list. Note the >> button. This button opens and closes more details about the parts list.

Adding Part Balloons

To add part balloons to your drawing view, select the Balloon or Balloon All tool from the Drawing Annotation Panel.

Parts List Text

The text in the parts list is controlled using the Drafting Standards (Format/Standard pull-down menu) dialog box. Under the Parts List tab you'll find the Text Style box. To create a text style, select Format/Text Styles and use the New button to create your own text style.

When you select the Balloon tool, you're prompted to select a location. This really means that you should select a part in a view. Once you've picked a part, the Parts List - Item Numbering dialog box appears. Usually you don't have to make any changes. Just pick OK to continue. An arrow appears on the part and a leader line is attached to the cursor. You can pick several points to define the leader. Once complete, right-click and select Continue. You can then place more balloons. Right-click again and select Done to stop.

When you select Balloon All, you're prompted to select a view. The balloons are then added automatically. They may not be in the correct positions, but you can pick and drag them into their proper positions.

Hands-On: Creating a Parts List and Adding Part Balloons

In this exercise, you're going to use the presentation views you created in the last Hands-On in this chapter. You're going to create a parts list and add part balloons to the bolt assembly.

1.   Open the boltassm presentation file that you previously created as shown in Figure 8.20.

2.   Start a new drawing by using the Ansi (in).idw template. Change the sheet size to B by right-clicking on Sheet:1 and selecting Edit Sheet. When the dialog box appears, change the size to B.

Figure 8.20
Assembly drawing

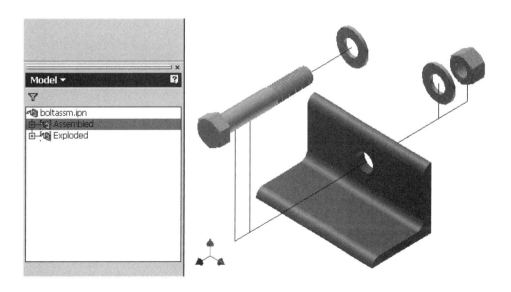

Figure 8.21
Drawing View dialog
box

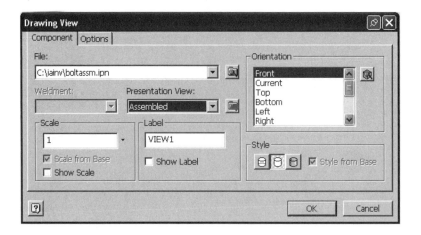

Adding Presentation Views

3.   Select the Base View tool from the Drawing Views Panel. The dialog box appears, similar to Figure 8.21. Because you already opened the presentation file, it's listed as the current file name. Match your settings to Figure 8.21. Note that the presentation view is set to Assembled. This means the presentation view named Assembled, which you created in the last Hands-On, is going to be used. Place the front view as shown in Figure 8.22.

4.   Use the Projected View tool to create the other two views shown in Figure 8.22.

5.   Select the Base View tool again. This time select the Exploded presentation view and the orientation should be set to Iso Top Right. Drag the isometric view into position and place it (see Figure 8.23).

Adding Part Balloons

6.   Open the Drawing Annotation Panel by picking on the Drawing Views Panel label.

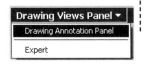

Figure 8.22   Base front view and two projected views

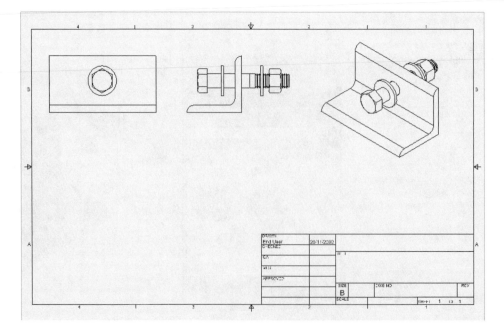

Figure 8.23
Exploded isometric view
added

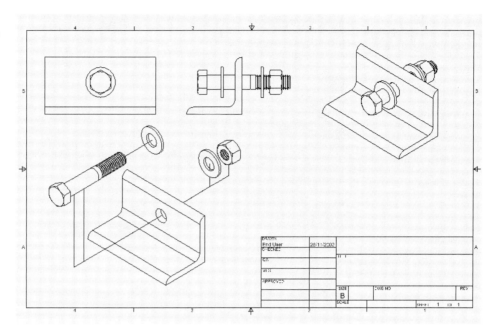

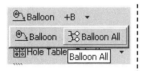

7.   Select the Balloon All tool and pick the exploded isometric view. When the Parts List - Item Numbering dialog box appears, pick OK. Part Ballons and leaders should automatically be placed. Refer to Figure 8.24 and pick and drag your balloons into similar positions.

Adding a Parts List

8.   Select the Parts List tool and Pick the exploded isometric view. Drag the parts list rectangle into position and place it (see Figure 8.25).

9.   Modify the parts list so that the part number column is removed and descriptions are added. Move your cursor over the parts list until it turns red. Right-click and select Edit Parts List from the context menu. The Edit Parts List dialog box appears, similar to Figure 8.26(a).

Select the Column Chooser tool and the Parts List Column Chooser dialog box appears as shown in Figure 8.26(b). Highlight Part Number in the Selected Properties column and pick the Remove button. This will remove Part Number

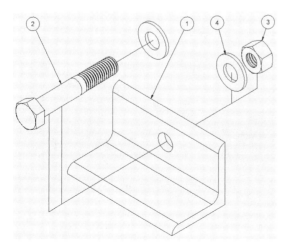

Figure 8.24   Part balloons added

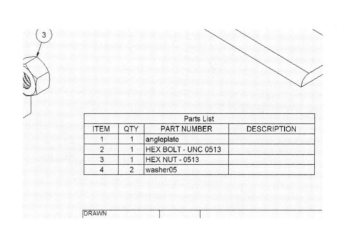

Parts List			
ITEM	QTY	PART NUMBER	DESCRIPTION
1	1	angleplate	
2	1	HEX BOLT - UNC 0513	
3	1	HEX NUT - 0513	
4	2	washer05	

Figure 8.25   Adding a parts list

Figure 8.26   Edit
Parts List and Parts List
Column Chooser dialog
boxes

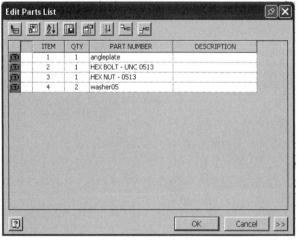

A

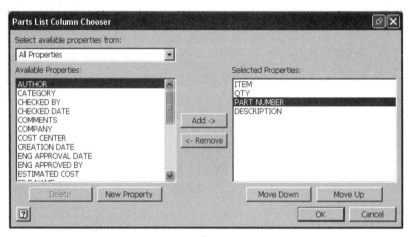

B

Figure 8.27   Adding
part descriptions

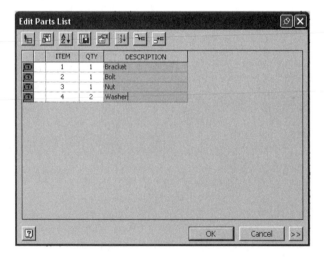

from the parts list. Select OK to return to the Edit Parts List dialog box. Fill in
the blank description boxes as shown in Figure 8.27. Pick OK and see the
results.

    10. Save your drawing as boltassm.

In a Nutshell

The culmination of your design is the assembly of the parts. To show this assembly in a drawing, you need to create presentation views. The presentation views control the placement and display of the parts. You can explode an assembly to show how the parts fit together. This can be done using an explosion factor or applying tweaks. You can create your drawing views from the presentation views that you have created.

Once the views have been placed, you can create a parts list and add part balloons to itemize and indicate the various parts.

You have come a long way in your journey from the creation of sketches to fully annotated assembly drawings. You should be able to apply what you have now learned to create almost any type of solid part and assembly.

 # Testing . . . testing . . . 1, 2, 3

Fill-in-the-Blanks

1. In the Select Assembly dialog box, you can enter a value of 0 for the explosion distance to _____ or enter a value greater than 0 to _____.

2. The explosion distance is _____.

3. A(n) _____ is used to indicate the intended travel of the part to its assembled position.

4. Moving a part around in the presentation view is called _____.

5. You must create a(n) _____ view first. Afterward, you can create _____, _____, and _____ assembly views.

True or False

6. The Column Chooser tool of the Edit Parts List dialog box allows you to select specific parts to be included on the parts list.   T or F

7. To add a part balloon, you can select the Place Balloon tool from the Symbol Standards dialog box.   T or F

Multiple Choice

8. You have two types of tweaks you can apply:
   a. move, transform
   b. move, rotate
   c. rotate, transform
   d. rotate, slide
   e. none of the above

9. The Bill of Materials is
   a. shortened to B.M.
   b. a list of building materials required for a project.
   c. an integral part of all Autodesk Inventor files.
   d. accessed through the Drawing Annotation panel.
   e. none of the above

What?

1. Describe the entire procedure for creating a new presentation view.

2. What is the difference between the procedure to create assembly views and the manner in which you create part views?

3. List and describe the two types of tweaks you can perform.

4. Why use a bill of materials?

5. What is the purpose of a parts balloon?

Let's Get Busy!

1. Create an assembly drawing of the sight glass assembly that you created in Chapter 7, Assignment 1. The drawing should look similar to Figure 8.28. Save your file as SGLASSAM.
2. Create an assembly drawing of the VBlock assembly that you created in Chapter 7, Assignment 2. The drawing should look similar to Figure 8.29. Save your file as VBLOCKAM.

Figure 8.28
Assembly drawing of
the sight glass

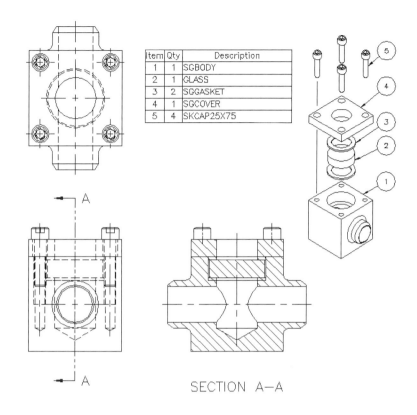

Item	Qty	Description
1	1	SGBODY
2	1	GLASS
3	2	SGGASKET
4	1	SGCOVER
5	4	SKCAP25X75

SECTION A—A

Figure 8.29
Assembly drawing of
the VBlock

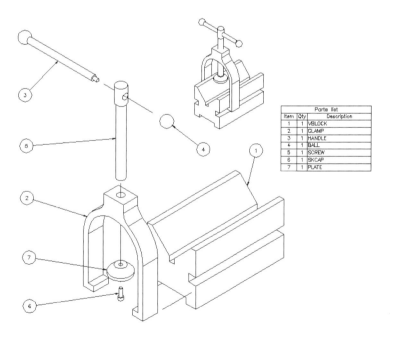

Parts list		
Item	Qty	Description
1	1	VBLOCK
2	1	CLAMP
3	1	HANDLE
4	1	BALL
5	1	SCREW
6	1	SKCAP
7	1	PLATE

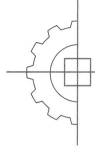

Appendix A

Installing CD-ROM Files

Setting up the files for this textbook is really quite easy. Using the following steps, you should have no problem getting started with your Autodesk Inventor learning.

Copying the Files

There is a Folder (subdirectory) called iainv located on the CD-ROM that comes with this book. Using Windows Explorer®, copy the folder and all its contents from the CD-ROM to your C: drive.

The iainv folder contains all the Hands-On Exercises required for this book, as well as two folders called Sglass and Vblock. The Sglass folder contains parts to be used in the assembly of a sight glass in Chapter 7. The Vblock folder contains parts to be used in the assembly of a Vblock in Chapter 7.

When you've finished copying, your Windows Explorer should have folders similar to Figure A.1 listed.

Whenever you're asked to open exercise files for the Hands-On, refer to these folders.

Figure A.1
Windows Explorer
showing iainv folder

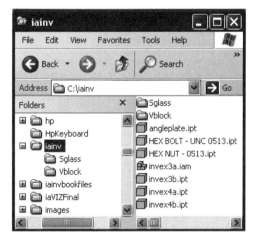

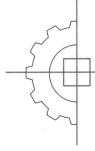

Appendix B

Reference Information

This appendix contains various reference information to help speed up your application of Autodesk Inventor. There are short-cut keys, comparisons between AutoCAD and Autodesk Inventor commands, and a list of what AutoCAD objects are translatable into Autodesk Inventor.

Autodesk Inventor Short-Cut Keys

The following are various keyboard combinations to activate Autodesk Inventor commands.

Key	Result
F1	Help for the active command or dialog box.
F2	Pans the graphics window.
F3	Zooms in or out in the graphics window.
F4	Rotates objects in the graphics window.
F5	Returns to the previous view.
B	Adds a balloon to a drawing.
C	Adds an assembly constraint.
D	Adds a dimension to a sketch or drawing.
E	Extrudes a profile.
F	Adds a feature control frame to a drawing.
H	Adds a hole feature.
L	Creates a line or arc.
O	Adds an ordinate dimension.
P	Places a component in the current assembly.
R	Creates a revolved feature.
S	Creates a sketch on a face or plane.
T	Tweaks a part in the current presentaton file.
Esc	Quits a command.
Delete	Deletes selected objects.
Backspace	In the active Line tool, removes the last sketched segment.
Alt + drag mouse	In assemblies, applies a mate constraint. In a sketch, moves spline shape points.
Crtl + Shift	Adds or removes objects from selection set.
Shift + right mouse click	Activates the Select tool menu.
Ctrl + Y	Activates Redo (revokes the last Undo).
Ctrl + Z	Activates Undo (revokes the last action).
Spacebar	When the 3D Rotate tool is active, switches between dynamic rotation and standard isometric and single plane views.

AutoCAD Command Comparison

Figures B.1 through B.4 show a comparison between various AutoCAD commands and their Autodesk Inventor equivalents. It should be noted that the commands are not always completely identical but are the closest matches available.

Figure B.1
AutoCAD 2D draw commands and their corresponding Autodesk Inventor sketch commands

AutoCAD	Autodesk Inventor
Line	Line
Polyline	Line
Polygon	Polygon
Rectangle	Two point rectangle
Arc	Three point arc
Circle	Center point circle
Spline	Spline
Ellipse	Ellipse
Point	Point, Hole center
Hatch	Fill, Hatch Sketch Region
Text	Text

Figure B.2
AutoCAD 2D modify commands and their corresponding Autodesk Inventor sketch commands

Erase		Delete key
Copy		Ctrl + C
Mirror	Mirror	
Offset	Offset	
Array	Circular Pattern	
	Rectangular Pattern	
Move	Move	
Rotate	Rotate	
Trim	Trim	
Extend	Extend	
Chamfer	Chamfer	
Fillet	Fillet	
Edit Spline		Click a fit point and drag
Edit Hatch		Right-click and choose Edit
Edit Text		Right-click and choose Edit

Figure B.3
AutoCAD Dimensioning commands and their corresponding Autodesk Inventor drawing commands

Ordinate Dimension   Ordinate Dimension

Quick Leader   Leader Text

Tolerance   Feature Control Frame

Center Mark   Center Mark

Figure B.4
AutoCAD 2D viewing commands and their corresponding Autodesk Inventor viewing commands

Pan Realtime   Pan

Zoom Realtime   Zoom

Zoom Window   Zoom Window

Zoom All   Zoom All

Zoom Previous   F5 key

Translation of AutoCAD Objects to Autodesk Inventor Objects

DWG data	Autodesk Inventor equivalent	DWG data	Autodesk Inventor equivalent
3D face	Not translated	Linear dimensions (horizontal, vertical, rotated, aligned)	Linear dimensions (horizontal, vertical, rotated, aligned)
3D solid	Not translated Note: 3D solids can be translated separately from 2D data.	Linetype	Linetype
		Mline	Line
Alternate units	Dual dimensions	Mtext	Sketch Text
Angular dimension	Angular dimension	Named view	Not translated
Arc	Arc	Ole2frame	Not translated
ASQUILTSURFACE	Not translated	Oleframe	Not translated
ASSURFACE	Not translated	Ordinate dimension	Ordinate dimension
Attribute (Attrib)	Prompted value	Part	Not translated
Attribute definition (Attdef)	Prompted value definitions	Point	Point
		Polyline (2D polyline)	Line
Augmented line	Line	Polyline (3D mesh)	Not translated
Block Definition	Sketched symbol resource	Polyline (3D polyline)	Not translated
Block Instance	Sketched symbol instance	Polyline (lightweight)	Line
Body	Not translated	Polyline (Polyface mesh)	Not translated
Circle	Circle	Proxy Object	Exploded and translated
Color	Color	Quilt, Quilted Surface	Not translated
Diameter dimension	Diameter dimension	Radius dimension	Radius dimension
Ellipse	Ellipse	Ray	Not translated
External reference (Xref)	Sketched symbol	Region	Not translated
		Shape	Hatch
Font change	Font override	Solid (2D)	Hatch
Group	Not translated	Spline	Spline
Hatch (Associative)	Hatch	Stitched surface	Not translated
Hatch (Not Associative)	Sketched symbol instance	Surface	Not translated
Layer	Not translated Note: Layer data is translated to sketches.	Text	Text
		Tiled viewport	Not translated
		Tolerance	Feature control frame
Layout	Sheet	Trace	Hatch
Leader	Callout symbol	Trimmed surface	Not translated
Leader arrowheads	Callout symbol leader arrowhead	User Coordinate System (UCS)	Not translated
Line	Line	Viewport (paper space)	Not translated
		Xline	Not translated

Appendix C

CAD Commands and Terms

The following tables list CAD commands, terms, and objects. They're not specific to Autodesk Inventor but more of a general nature. They're here for those who are new to CAD and aren't familiar with some of the basic terms. Those of you who have been using another CAD program such as AutoCAD will already be familiar with these terms.

CAD Commands/ Terms	Description
Array	An array is a number of copied objects in a rectangular or circular pattern. For rectangular arrays you control the number of rows and columns and the distance between each. For circular arrays, you control the number of copies of the object and whether the copies are rotated. To create many regularly spaced objects, arraying is faster than copying.
Chamfer	A chamfer is a flattened or beveled corner where two lines meet.
Copy	Copy allows you to create duplicates of objects at a specified distance from the original. You specify the distance and direction by two points: (a) from point (1) and (a) to point (2), called the base point and the second point of displacement, respectively. These points can be located anywhere within the drawing.
Dimensions	Dimensions are numerical descriptions of the distances between specified points on a drawing. Linear dimensions can be horizontal, vertical, or aligned. With aligned dimensions, the dimension line is parallel to the line (imaginary or real) between the extension line origins. Baseline (or parallel) and continued (or chain) dimensions are a series of consecutive dimensions that are based on a linear dimension. Radial dimensions measure the radii and diameters of arcs and circles with optional centerlines or a centermark.
Ellipse	The shape of an ellipse is determined by two axes that define its length and width. The longer axis is called the major axis; the shorter one is the minor axis.
Erase	You can remove objects from your drawing using several methods, including erasing them, cutting them to Clipboard, or pressing Del.
Extend	You can extend objects so they end precisely at boundary edges defined by other objects.
Extrude	You can extrude planar faces along a path, or you can specify a height value and a tapered angle. Each face has a positive side, which is the side in the direction of the face's normal (the current face you're working on). Entering a positive value extrudes the face in its positive direction (usually outward); a negative value extrudes in the negative direction (usually inward).

CAD Commands/ Terms	Description
Grid	The grid is a rectangular pattern of dots or lines that extends over the drawing area. Using the grid is similar to placing a sheet of grid paper under a drawing. The grid helps you align objects and visualize the distances between them. The grid is not plotted. If you zoom in or out of your drawing, you may need to adjust grid spacing to be more appropriate for the new magnification.
Hatch	Many drafting applications use a process called hatching to fill an area with a pattern. The pattern is used to differentiate components of a project or to signify the material composing an object.
Leader	A leader object typically consists of an arrowhead, a leader line or curve, and a multiline text object.
Mirror	Mirroring creates a mirror image of objects. It is useful for creating symmetrical objects because you can quickly draw half the object and then mirror it instead of drawing the entire object.
Move	You can move objects without changing their orientation or size. By using coordinates, you can move objects with precision.
Offset	Offsetting creates a new object whose shape parallels the shape of a selected object. Offsetting a circle or an arc creates a larger or smaller circle or arc, depending on which side you specify for the offset.
Pan	You can shift the location of your view by using Pan. You pan dynamically by picking and dragging your pointing device. Like panning with a camera, Pan does not change the location or magnification of objects on your drawing; it changes only the view.
Plot	Plots/prints a drawing to a plotter, printer, or file.
Pull-down Menu	Pull-down menus typically lie at the top of the application window. By picking on a menu heading, a list of menu items is pulled down onto the screen; move your cursor along the list to pick the desired command.
Redo	You can reverse the effects of Undo.
Revolve	With Revolve, you can create a solid by revolving a closed object about an axis.
Rotate	You can rotate objects around a specified point. To determine the angle of rotation, you enter an angle value.
Solid Modeling	Solid modeling is the easiest type of 3D modeling to use. With a solid modeler, you can make 3D objects by generating basic 3D shapes—boxes, cones, cylinders, spheres, wedges, and tori (donuts)—and then combining these shapes to create more complex solids by joining or subtracting them or finding their intersecting (overlapping) volume. You can also create solids by sweeping a 2D object along a path or revolving it about an axis. You can also define solids parametrically and maintain associativity between 3D models and the 2D views that you generate from them.

CAD Commands/ Terms	**Description**
Toolbars	Toolbars contain buttons that start commands. When you move the pointing device over a toolbar button, the tooltip displays the name of the button. Buttons with a small black triangle in the lower-right corner have flyouts that contain related commands. With the cursor over the icon, hold down the pick button until the flyout appears.
Trim	You can trim objects so that they end precisely at boundary edges defined by other objects.
Undo	You can backtrack your recent actions using Undo. This command can work in successive jumps.
Zoom	You can change the magnification of a view by zooming in and out. Like zooming in and out with a camera, Zoom does not change the absolute size of objects in the drawing; it changes only the magnification of the view.

CAD Objects	**Description**
Arc	An arc line with different beginning and endpoints and a constant radius.
Circle	A continuous arc line with the same start and endpoints and a constant radius.
Fillet	Filleting connects two objects with a smoothly fitted arc of a specified radius.
Line	A series of contiguous line segments. Each single line segment can be edited separately from the other line segments in a series.
Polygon	Polygons are closed lines with between 3 and 120 equal-length sides. Creating polygons is a simple way to draw squares, equilateral triangles, octagons, and so on.
Rectangle	Draws a series of lines in a rectangular shape.
Text	When you create single-line text, you assign a text style and set alignment. The text style sets the default characteristics of the text object. The alignment determines what part of the text character aligns with the insertion point.

Index

T

U

V

W